Executive Summary

"Unfortunately, many Americans live on the outskirts of hope—some because of their poverty, and some because of their color, and all too many because of both. Our task is to help replace their despair with opportunity. This administration today, here and now, declares unconditional war on poverty in America. I urge this Congress and all Americans to join with me in that effort."

- *President Lyndon B. Johnson, January 8, 1964*

Fifty years ago, in January of 1964, President Lyndon B. Johnson declared a "War on Poverty" and introduced initiatives designed to improve the education, health, skills, jobs, and access to economic resources of those struggling to make ends meet. While there is more work to do, in the ensuing decades we have strengthened and reformed many of these programs and had significant success in reducing poverty. In this report, the Council of Economic Advisers presents evidence of the progress made possible by decades of bipartisan efforts to fight poverty by expanding economic opportunity and rewarding hard work. We also document some of the key steps the Obama Administration has taken to further increase opportunity and economic security by improving key programs while ensuring greater efficiency and integrity. These steps prevented millions of hardworking Americans from slipping into poverty during the worst economic crisis since the Great Depression.

❖ *Poverty has declined by more than one-third since 1967.*

➢ The percent of the population in poverty when measured to include tax credits and other benefits has declined from 25.8 percent in 1967 to 16.0 percent in 2012.

➢ These figures use new historical estimates of the Census Bureau's Supplemental Poverty Measure (SPM) anchored to today's poverty thresholds. The SPM is widely acknowledged to measure poverty more accurately than the official poverty measure, which excludes the value of refundable tax credits and benefits like nutrition assistance and has other limitations.

➢ By anchoring the measure to today's poverty standards we are able to ask how many people in each year since 1967 would have had inflation-adjusted family resources below the 2012 SPM poverty thresholds.

❖ *Despite real progress in the War on Poverty, there is more work to do.*

➢ In 2012, there were 49.7 million Americans grappling with the economic and social hardships of living below the poverty line, including 13.4 million children.

➢ While the United States is often seen as the land of economic opportunity, only about half of low-income Americans make it out of the lowest income distribution quintile over a 20-year period. About 40 percent of the differences in parents' income are

2

reflected in children's income as they become adults, pointing to strong lingering effects from growing up in poverty.

❖ *This significant decline in poverty is largely due to programs that have historically enjoyed bipartisan support and increase economic security and opportunity.*

➢ A measure of "market poverty," that reflects what the poverty rate would be without any tax credits or other benefits, rose from 27.0 percent to 28.7 percent between 1967 and 2012. Countervailing forces of increasing levels of education on the one hand, and inequality, wage stagnation, and a declining minimum wage on the other resulted in "market poverty" increasing slightly over this period. However, poverty measured taking antipoverty and social insurance programs into account fell by more than a third, highlighting the essential role that these programs have played in fighting poverty.

➢ Programs designed to increase economic security and opportunity lifted over 45 million people from poverty in 2012, and led to an average of 27 million people lifted out of poverty per year for 45 years between 1968 and 2012. Cumulatively these efforts prevented 1.2 billion "person years" of poverty over this period.

➢ Social Security has played a crucial role in lowering poverty among the elderly. Poverty among those aged 65 and older was 35 percent in 1960. Following rapid expansions in Social Security in the 1960s and 1970s, poverty among the elderly fell to 14.8 percent in 2012.

➢ These programs are especially important in mitigating poverty during recessions. Despite an increase in "market poverty" of 4.5 percentage points between 2007 and 2010, the poverty rate, appropriately measured, rose only 0.5 percentage points due to both existing programs and immediate actions taken by President Obama when he took office in response to the worst financial crisis since the Great Depression.

"Deep poverty"—defined as the fraction of individuals living below 50 percent of the poverty line has declined as a result of these programs. Without government tax credits or other benefits, 19.2 percent of the U.S. population would have been in deep poverty in 2012, but only 5.3 percent were in deep poverty when these benefits are included.

❖ *Programs that strengthen economic security and increase opportunity continue to be essential in keeping millions of Americans out of poverty and helping them work their way into the middle class.*

➢ Social Security benefits reduced the 2012 poverty rate by 8.5 percentage points among all individuals, and by 39.9 percentage points among those aged 65 or older.

> Tax credits such as the Earned Income Tax Credit (EITC) and Child Tax Credit (CTC) reduced the 2012 poverty rate by 3.0 percentage points among all individuals, and by 6.7 percentage points among children.

> The Supplemental Nutrition Assistance Program (SNAP)—formerly known as the Food Stamp Program—reduced poverty in 2012 by 1.6 percentage points among all individuals, and by 3.0 percentage points among children.

> Unemployment Insurance (UI) reduced poverty by 0.8 percentage points in 2012.

❖ *Antipoverty programs have been increasingly oriented around rewarding and encouraging work and are an important source of opportunity for low-income working families.*

> Both the EITC and the partially refundable component of the CTC increase the reward to work, offsetting payroll taxes and providing a supplement to labor market earnings. Research has shown this increases work and earnings, and increases participation in the workforce, particularly for single parents.

> Some traditional antipoverty programs have been redesigned to encourage and promote work. The vast majority of Americans receiving nutrition assistance have a job or are either too young to work, are over age 65 or are disabled. Meanwhile, bipartisan welfare reform signed by President Clinton in 1996 strengthened work requirements and put a greater emphasis on employment.

> Despite concerns that antipoverty programs may discourage employment, the best research suggests that work disincentive effects are small or nonexistent for most programs.

❖ *Programs that help fight poverty and provide economic security touch a wide swath of Americans at some point in their lives.*

> Programs that fight poverty help a broad range of Americans get back on their feet after economic misfortune. For example, about half of taxpayers with children used the EITC at some point between 1979 and 2006, and over two-thirds of Americans aged 14 to 22 in 1979 received income from SNAP, AFDC/TANF, Supplemental Security Income (SSI) or UI at some point between 1978 and 2010.

> Social Security Old Age and Survivors' Insurance, Social Security Disability Insurance, and UI are available to all Americans with a steady work history. These social insurance programs play an important role in keeping out of poverty those who retire, experience a work-limiting disability, lose a parent or spouse, or lose a job through no fault of their own.

❖ *The economic and social benefits from these programs go beyond just helping reduce poverty in the current generation.*

  ➢ Increased access to SNAP for children has been found to lead to better health and greater economic self-sufficiency in adulthood.

  ➢ Increased family income in childhood from the EITC and CTC leads to higher student achievement.

  ➢ The long-term effects of Head Start and other high-quality preschool programs include higher educational attainment, employment, and earnings, and lower rates of teen pregnancy and crime, as beneficiary children become teenagers and young adults.

❖ *President Obama's policies to restore economic security and increase opportunity have helped reduce poverty.*

  ➢ The Affordable Care Act ensures all Americans have access to quality, affordable health insurance, by providing the resources and flexibility states need to expand their Medicaid programs to all people who are in or near poverty as well as financial help so hardworking families can find a health plan that fits their needs and their budgets.

  ➢ The President significantly expanded the refundability of the Child Tax Credit, making it available to millions of working parents who were previously ineligible. He also expanded the EITC for larger families, who face disproportionately high poverty rates, and for low-income married couples. Together these expansions benefit approximately 15 million families by an average of $800 per year. The President is proposing to make these tax credit improvements permanent and also to raise the minimum wage.

  ➢ The Administration has advanced investments in early learning and development programs and reforms for coordinated State early learning systems. President Obama has proposed the expansion of voluntary home visiting programs for pregnant women and families with young children; Early Head Start-Child Care Partnerships to improve the quality of care for infants and toddlers; and high-quality preschool for every child.

  ➢ President Obama has advanced reforms of the nation's K-12 education system to support higher standards that will prepare students to succeed in college and the workplace; pushed efforts to recruit, prepare, develop, and advance effective teachers and principals; and encouraged a national effort to turn around our lowest-achieving schools. The Administration has also put forward proposals to redesign the Nation's high schools to better engage students and to connect 99 percent of students to high-speed broadband and digital learning tools within the next five years.

  ➢ President Obama has proposed Promise Zones where businesses partner with local communities hit hard by the recession to put people back to work and communities can develop and implement their own sustainable plans for a continuum of family and community services and comprehensive education reforms.

➢ President Obama has proposed increased employment and training opportunities for adults who are low-income or long-term unemployed, and summer and year-round opportunities for youth along with reforms to our unemployment system to make it more of a re-employment system, and community college initiatives to reform our higher education system and support training partnerships with business in high-demand industries.

➢ Other achievements include making college more affordable by reforming student loan programs, raising the maximum Pell Grant, and establishing the American Opportunity Tax Credit which is the first partially refundable tax credit for college; placing 372,000 low-income youth into summer and year-round employment in 2009 and 2010; improving access to school meal programs that help children learn and thrive; and extending minimum wage and overtime protections to nearly all home care workers to help make their jobs more financially rewarding.

The fundamental lesson of the past 50 years is that we have made progress in the War on Poverty largely through bipartisan efforts to strengthen economic security and increase opportunity. As our economy moves forward, rather than cut these programs and risk leaving hardworking Americans behind, we need to build on the progress we have made to strengthen and reform them. Going forward, we can't lose sight of the positive part government can continue to play in reducing economic hardship and ensuring access to economic opportunity for all citizens. At the same time, sustainable improvements are only possible if we create jobs and speed the economic recovery in the short run, raise economic growth in the long run, and work to ensure that the benefits of a growing economy reach all Americans.

I.   Measuring Poverty: Who is Poor in America?

"We must open our eyes and minds to the poverty in our midst ."
1964 Economic Report of the President.

Michael Harrington's influential 1962 book *The Other America* depicted the poor as inhabiting an "invisible land," a world described in the 1964 *Economic Report of the President* as "scarcely recognizable, and rarely recognized, by the majority of their fellow Americans." One early achievement of Johnson's War on Poverty was to cast light on the problem of poverty by developing an official poverty measure that has been released by the government in each year since August 1969.[1] While reasonable at the time, this measure has turned out to be ill-suited to capturing the progress subsequently made in the War. As a result, modern poverty measures tell a different story of who is poor, and especially how this has changed over time.

Measuring Poverty

Measuring poverty is not a simple task; even defining it is controversial. Just starting with a commonsense definition of the poor—"those whose basic needs exceed their means to satisfy them"—requires difficult conceptual choices regarding what constitutes basic needs and what resources should be counted in figuring a family's means. There are no generally accepted standards of minimum needs for most necessary consumption items such as housing, clothing, transportation, etc. Moreover, our ideas about minimum needs may change over time. For example, in 1963 even some middle-income households did not have hot and cold running water indoors. Today, over 99 percent of households of all income levels have complete indoor plumbing.

The Official Poverty Measure

Mollie Orshansky, an economist in the Social Security Administration, developed the official poverty thresholds between 1963 and 1964 (Fisher 1992). At the time, the Department of Agriculture had a set of food plans derived using data from the 1955 Household Food Consumption Survey, the lowest cost of which was deemed adequate for "temporary or emergency use when funds are low." Because families in this survey spent about one-third of their incomes, on average, on food, Orshansky set the poverty threshold at three times the dollar cost of this "economy food plan," with adjustments for family size, composition, and whether the family lived on a farm.

---

[1] A similar poverty measure was adopted internally by the Office of Economic Opportunity in 1965.

These income thresholds that were first used as the poverty thresholds for the 1963 calendar year have served as the basis for the official poverty thresholds ever since. These dollar amounts have been adjusted for inflation to hold the real value of the income needed to be above poverty the same over time. There have been minor tweaks to the methodology involving which price index is used to adjust for inflation, and how adjustments are made for family structure and farm status.

FLAWS IN THE OFFICIAL POVERTY MEASURE

The official poverty measure (OPM) has several flaws that distort our understanding of both the level of poverty and how it has changed over time. Perhaps the most significant problem with the OPM is its measure of family resources, based on pre-tax income plus cash transfers (like cash welfare, social security, or UI payments), but not taxes, tax credits, or non-cash transfers. As such it inhabits a measurement limbo between "market poverty" (based on pre-tax, pre-transfer resources) and "post-tax, post transfer poverty" reflecting well-being after taking into account the impact of policies directed at the poor.

Several other shortcomings are more technical. First, the dollar value defining the cost of basic needs, or the poverty threshold, was set in the 1960s and has been updated each year since using an index of food prices at first, but then the Consumer Price Index (CPI) after 1969. The use of the CPI is one source of the problems with the official measure that limits its usefulness for historical comparison. Methodological advances in measuring prices (e.g., rental equivalence treatment of housing costs, quality adjustments for some large purchases, and geometric averaging for similar goods) have shown that the CPI overstated inflation substantially prior to the early 1980s, leading to an inflated estimate of the cost of basic needs and thus higher measured poverty over time. Revising the OPM measure using the CPI-U-RS (a historical series estimated consistently using modern methods) results in a fall in poverty from 1966 to 2012 that is 3 percentage points greater than that depicted by the official measure. Another flaw with the OPM thresholds is that they do not accurately reflect geographic variation in costs of living or economies associated with family size and structure.

All current income-based poverty measures, including both the OPM and the SPM, suffer from large underreporting of both incomes and benefits. For example, Meyer, Mok, and Sullivan (2009) show that in 1984, March CPS respondents reported only 75 percent of AFDC/TANF dollars, and this fell to 49 percent in 2004. For SNAP benefits, which are accounted for in the SPM but not the OPM, 71 percent of the value was reported in 1984 compared to 57 percent in 2004. Underreporting will tend to increase measured poverty, so increases in underreporting over time understate the decline in the poverty rate during this period. The underreporting also means that the estimated effects of government programs on poverty, as described in section III, are likely to be conservative lower-bound estimates of the true effects.

In defining the family resources to be compared to the poverty line, Orshansky created the thresholds to be applied to after-tax money income—the income concept used in the 1955 Household Food Consumption Survey. However, she was forced to use pre-tax money income (including cash transfer payments) due to limitations in the Current Population Survey (CPS) data, the only source of nationally representative information on income. At the time, this was an adequate approximation of disposable income, as few low-income families had any federal income tax liability or credits owed, and in-kind transfers were not a quantitatively important feature of the safety net.

The Supplemental Poverty Measure

While Orshansky's measure provided a reasonable depiction of poverty in the 1960s, it has not aged well.[2] Today, for example, the value of the two largest non-health programs directing aid to the poor—the EITC and SNAP—are entirely ignored by the official measure, making it impossible to assess the success of these tools in fighting poverty. Over the past five decades, researchers have pointed to many flaws in the official measure (see box), leading to the development of alternative measures of poverty with more comprehensive measures of both family needs and resources. The Census Bureau created a Supplemental Poverty Measure (SPM), which departs dramatically from the official measure in its methodology for calculating both the poverty thresholds and family resources.[3] This measure, first published in 2011, calculates poverty thresholds using recent expenditures by families at the 33rd percentile of the expenditure distribution on an array of necessary items, including food, shelter, clothing, and utilities.[4] The dollar amount is calculated separately for families depending on whether they own or rent their home and whether they have a mortgage, and then increased by 20 percent to allow for other necessary expenses. Further adjustments are made based on differences in family size and structure, and, unlike in the official measure, the threshold is adjusted for geographic variation in living costs (Short 2013).

The Supplemental Poverty Measure also uses a more accurate measure of disposable income that accounts for both a greater number of income sources and a wider array of necessary expenditures. Unlike the official measure, the SPM uses a post-tax, post-transfer concept of resources that adds to family earnings all cash transfers and the cash-equivalent of in-kind transfers such as food assistance (for example, SNAP or free lunch) minus net tax liabilities, which can be negative for families receiving refundable tax credits like the EITC or CTC. Necessary expenditures on work and child-care are then subtracted from resources.

---

[2] It should be noted that Orshansky herself noted many flaws with her measure, and believed it understated poverty. She argued it measured income inadequacy rather than adequacy, stating "if it is not possible to state unequivocally 'how much is enough,' it should be possible to assert with confidence how much, on an average, is too little (Orshansky 1965)."

[3] While we use the term 'family' here, the SPM differs in its definition of a 'family unit' when assuming the unit of individuals over which resources are shared. Most importantly, the SPM includes all related individuals living at the same address, but also cohabiting individuals and co-residing children in their care.

[4] More accurately, the thresholds are based on average expenditures on food, clothing, shelter, and utilities between the 30th and 36th percentiles of that distribution, multiplied by 1.2 to account for other necessary expenses and adjusted for geographic differences in cost of living and family size and structure.

The Supplemental Poverty Measure also subtracts medical-out-of-pocket (MOOP) expenses from families' resources since those funds are not available to meet other needs. The SPM can thus be thought of as a measure of deprivation with respect to non-health care goods and services.[5] However, it does not provide an accurate picture of the benefits of health care. Instead, the SPM values health insurance only insofar as it reduces households' out-of-pocket medical costs and thus frees up resources for other uses. It misses benefits that may arise because insurance improves access to health care and may therefore improve health outcomes, or reduces stress caused by exposure to financial risk. As a result, the measured trend in SPM poverty may understate progress in decreasing economic hardship since the War on Poverty began by ignoring these benefits of increased access to insurance.

One important feature of the Supplemental Poverty Measure design is that the definition of minimum needs is adjusted each year based on recent data on family expenditures on necessities rather than adjusting a fixed bundle only for inflation. By considering families' expenditures on an array of necessary items, including food, shelter, clothing, and utilities—and then setting poverty rates based on how much families at the 33rd percentile spend—the SPM adjusts poverty thresholds as societies' spending patterns on these necessities shifts.[6] This type of threshold is "quasi-relative," in the sense that thresholds will tend to rise with income, but are not directly tied to income as in a purely relative definition of poverty, such as setting a threshold at half the median household income.

Alternatively, it is possible to create an "anchored" version of the Supplemental Poverty Measure, which is the focus in this report. The anchored version, like the official measure, fixes poverty thresholds based on expenditures on necessary items in a given year and then adjusts only for inflation in each year. This version allows for the use of the more comprehensive definition of resources in measuring poverty over time, while setting a fixed assessment of what constitutes basic needs spending on food, shelter, clothing, and utilities. The anchored measure is also more consistent with the vision of the War on Poverty architects, who believed that poverty can be eradicated. Eliminating poverty defined with a relative measure may be nearly impossible, as the threshold rises apace with incomes.[7]

---

[5] Korenman and Remler (2013) argue that the SPM's treatment of MOOP expenses actually does a poor job of capturing even deprivation of non-health care goods and services. They argue that households that are able to spend a large amount on health care are frequently those with substantial savings or other resources to draw on, and they present evidence that households with high out-of-pocket expenses frequently score lower on "direct" measures of hardship, like food insecurity.

[6] So, for example, if families across the income spectrum spend more on, say, housing because preferences for or the ability to pay for space or bathrooms change then what is considered necessary for minimum housing will change.

[7] The SPM is a hybrid, "quasi-relative" measure such that when spending on necessities increases, the threshold defining who is poor also increases. Eliminating poverty is theoretically possible, but it depends on how a country's spending on necessities evolves as its income increases and requires spending on these goods to be stable even as income grows.

Who is Poor?

In an attempt to "provide an understanding of the enemy" for Johnson's War, the 1964 *Economic Report of the President* presented tables depicting the "topography of poverty." As Table 1 shows, some of the landmarks have changed since 1960 while many remain the same. For 2012, the Table presents the poverty rates measured with both the official poverty measure and the supplemental poverty measure.[8] The official measure is displayed for comparing the relative poverty of various groups in the two time periods, but should not be used for comparing changes in the levels of poverty between the two time periods due to the flaws in the official measure discussed above. The next section will provide trend data using a consistent measure. Since historical estimates of the SPM are available only starting in 1967, the table shows only official poverty rates for 1959 using the 1960 Census.

Table 1

Poverty Rates by Selected Characteristics

	1959	2012	
	Official Poverty Measure	Official Poverty Measure	Supplemental Poverty Measure
All people	22.4	15.1	16.0
Household characteristics			
Head worked last year	17.8	10.0	10.5
Head did not work last year	55.7	27.4	29.2
Head married	18.9	7.9	10.2
Head single female	47.4	29.1	28.9
Individual Characteristics			
Less than high school (age 25-64)	25.3	33.9	35.8
High school (age 25-64)	10.2	15.6	17.5
College (adults 25-64)	6.7	4.5	5.9
Less than 18	26.8	22.3	18.0
65 years and older	36.9	9.1	14.8
Female	24.9	16.4	16.7
African American	57.8	27.3	25.8
Hispanic	40.5	25.8	27.8
Asian	N/A	11.8	16.7
Native Alaskans/American Indians	N/A	34.2	30.3
White	19.5	9.8	10.7
Immigrant	23.0	19.3	25.4
Disabled (age 18-64)	N/A	28.4	26.5
Lives outside a metropolitan area	47.4	17.9	13.9

Note: Calculations based on characteristics of household heads exclude people living in group quarters.

Source: CEA calculations based on 1960 Census and U.S. Census Bureau.

---

[8] In this table we use the official Supplemental Poverty Measure statistics published by the Census Bureau (Short 2013), whereas for historical comparisons below we rely on historical estimates produced by Wimer et al. (2013), described below. The series from Wimer et al. anchors its poverty measure at the 2012 SPM thresholds, so their estimated poverty rates for 2012 are very similar to those in Table 1.

Employment

Unsurprisingly, unemployment is one of the strongest predictors of poverty. In 1959, 55.7 percent of individuals in households where the head was out of work for a full year were poor—three times the rate of individuals in households where the head worked at least one week during the year. While this rate has declined to 29.2 percent, individuals in households where the head was out of work for a full-year were still three times as likely to be poor as those in households where the head worked.

However, even full-time employment is not enough to keep all families out of poverty today. A person working full-time, full-year in 2013 being paid the minimum wage earns $14,500 for the year. These earnings alone leave such workers below the poverty threshold if they have even one child. While the EITC, SNAP, and other benefits will help pull a family of two above the poverty line, for a larger family—such as one with three children—full-time, full-year minimum wage work combined with government assistance is unlikely to be enough to lift that family out of poverty.

Education Level

Education's role in poverty prevention has become more important over time: in 1959, high-school dropouts were 3.8 times more likely to be poor than college graduates; but in 2012, they were 6.1 times more likely to be poor (based on the SPM measure). The growth in the poverty gap by education is driven by growth in earnings inequality, which has led to much greater earnings for college graduates than for those with less education.

Children

As in 1959, the child poverty rate today is higher than the poverty rate of the overall population, though the SPM shows that children are disproportionately helped by our poverty-fighting programs. Once taxes and in-kind transfers are taken into account, the gap between child and non-child poverty falls. According to the official measure, the child poverty rate in 2012 was 22.3 percent—nearly 48 percent higher than the overall rate. But the official rate ignores the contributions of the most important antipoverty programs for children: the EITC and other refundable tax credits and SNAP. Including the value of these resources, the SPM estimates that 18 percent of children are poor, a rate that is 12.5 percent (2 percentage points) higher than the overall poverty rate.

The Elderly

One of the most heralded successes of the War on Poverty is the large reduction in elderly poverty rates. In 1959, poverty rates were highest among the elderly with 36.9 percent of people 65 and older living in poverty (based on OPM). Today poverty rates of those 65 and older are below the national average. Using the SPM measure shows elderly poverty at 14.8 percent, however, more than 50 percent higher than the OPM measure. The reason for this difference is that the SPM subtracts expenditures on medical expenses from a family's resources, and the elderly tend to have much higher medical expenses. Indeed, if the out-of-pocket medical costs were not subtracted, the measured elderly poverty rate would be only 8.4

percent—*lower* than their official poverty rate of 9.1 percent.[9] In the absence of Medicare and Medicaid, out-of-pocket medical expenses of the elderly would almost certainly cause their poverty to be much higher than the SPM poverty rate of 14.8 percent.

Women

Women are more likely than men to be in poverty, with a 2012 poverty rate of 16.7 percent compared to 15.3 percent among men. This gap largely reflects higher poverty among single women, both those age 18-64 (22.9 percent compared to 20.2 percent among single men) and those age 65 or older (21.2 percent compared to 16.1 percent among single men).

Childcare responsibilities help explain the poverty gap for single working-age women. Almost one-third (31.0 percent) of single women age 18-64 lived with their children in 2012, among whom the poverty rate was 27.5 percent. Just over one-third (35.2 percent) of single mothers age 18-64 were employed full-time, full-year in 2012, compared to 44.6 percent of single working-age males and 43.3 percent of single working-age women without children at home. Increased support for childcare for young children has been shown to positively affect mothers' employment hours and earnings (Connelly and Kimmel 2003; Misra et al. 2011). The high poverty rate among older single women relative to men reflects a combination of lower Social Security benefits due to lower lifetime earnings; lower rates of pension coverage; and greater longevity that increases the chances of outliving their private savings (Anzick and Weaver 2001, SSA 2012).

Race and Ethnicity

Poverty rates have fallen for all racial and ethnic groups over time and gaps by race have shrunk slightly. However, troubling gaps still remain. In 1959, nearly three-fifths of African Americans were in poverty, which was nearly three times the poverty rate of Whites. The fraction of African Americans in poverty has fallen by more than half since then; yet at 25.8 percent, the SPM poverty rate for African Americans is still more than double the rate of 10.7 percent for Whites. Today, the SPM poverty rate among Hispanics is 27.8 percent, similar to that among African Americans. However, this reflects smaller declines in poverty among Hispanics over the past 50 years. Among both African Americans and Hispanics the official and supplemental poverty rates tell similar stories. However, the SPM reveals that Asian Americans have a slightly higher poverty rate than the national average—at 16.7 percent—whereas their OPM poverty rate is lower than the national average. The higher SPM rate for Asian Americans reflects, in part, the fact that they tend to live in high-cost metropolitan areas (e.g., Los Angeles, New York City, etc.) and the SPM poverty thresholds are higher in such places due to its geographic adjustments for cost of living. Finally, while we do not have measures of poverty among American Indians and Alaska Natives in the earlier period, currently they have the highest rates of poverty of any race and ethnicity group at 30.3 percent in 2012.

---

[9] Accounting for out-of-pocket medical expenses raises measured poverty for nonelderly adults and children by 2.9 and 3.1 percentage points, respectively.

People with Disabilities

Over one-fourth of working-age people with disabilities are estimated to live in poverty, using both the OPM (28.4 percent) and SPM (26.5 percent) measures. This largely reflects their low employment rates. The effective poverty rate of people with disabilities may be understated due to the extra costs that often accompany disability, such as for home and vehicle renovations, assistive equipment, personal assistance, and other items and services that may not be covered by insurance or government programs (Sen 2009: 258, She and Livermore 2007, Fremstad 2009, Schur et al. 2013: 32-33).

Rural and Urban Communities

The official poverty measure overestimates rural poverty since rural communities tend to have lower costs of living than urban areas and the official measure does not take geographic cost-of-living differences into account. However, the OPM has revealed that significant poverty persists in rural communities throughout the country today. The Economic Research Service of the U.S. Department of Agriculture estimates that eighty-five percent of persistent poverty counties—counties that have been in high poverty (over 20 percent based on the OPM) for at least 30 years—are in rural areas. The gap between poverty rates outside and within metropolitan areas, though, has narrowed since 1959, when poverty rates outside metropolitan areas were more than double the rates within these areas. In fact, the adjustments for different housing costs across geographic areas in the SPM show that poverty rates are higher in metropolitan areas than in rural areas today.[10]

---

[10] This comparison may be affected by significant differences among geographic areas in costs other than housing, such as transportation. In addition, there may be differences in housing quality that are not captured by the differences in housing costs.

II.   Assessing the War on Poverty

"The elimination of income poverty is usefully thought of as a one-time operation in pursuit of a goal unique to this generation. That goal should be achieved before 1980, at which time the next generation will have set new economic and social goals, perhaps including a new distributional goal for themselves"

- *Robert Lampman, CEA economist in the Johnson Administration, writing in 1971.*

This section presents new historical estimates of the poverty rate from 1967 to 2012 based on the Supplemental Poverty Measure and shows that substantial progress has been made in reducing poverty since President Johnson began major policy initiatives as part of his fight against poverty. In the past 45 years, the poverty rate fell from 25.8 to 16.0 percent—a reduction of over one-third. The CEA documents that much of this decline was due to the increased poverty-reducing effects of the safety net expansion set in motion during the Johnson Administration. Based on a measure of pre-tax, pre-transfer income, the poverty rate would be about as high today as in 1967: over 28 percent. These analyses show that safety net programs lifted 45 million people from poverty in 2012, and between 1968 and 2012 prevented 1.2 billion "person years" from living below the poverty line. This section first reviews changes in the economy that provide context for understanding the lack of growth in market incomes in the bottom part of the distribution over this time period. The section then presents estimates of poverty trends since 1967 measured using modern methods.

Context

As noted in the quote beginning this section, the architects of the War on Poverty were confident they would live to see poverty eradicated. Looking at the data at their disposal at the time, it is easy to see how an analyst might have believed the end of poverty was on the horizon. Figure 1 shows the trend in the official poverty measure—the only consistently available measure tracking poverty until recently—from 1959 through 2012. Based on the trend in poverty observed between 1959 and 1968, one would have indeed forecast—extrapolating linearly—that poverty would be eradicated by 1980. Poverty fell by a remarkably consistent rate of about 1.15 percentage points a year over that 10-year period, but the official poverty measure stopped declining afterwards, reaching its lowest point in 1973.

As previously noted, the OPM is a measure of cash income that does not include non-cash benefits or tax credits. While it does not accurately capture the trend in poverty over time, it is nonetheless worth considering why the improvement in this measure of cash income slowed so abruptly in the early 1970s. The first, and clearest, answer is that Social Security expansions during the 1960s brought the rate of poverty among the elderly down rapidly before leveling in the 1970s (Engelhardt and Gruber 2006). In 1959, 36.9 percent of those 65 and older were in poverty, but by 1974 that fraction had fallen to 14.6 percent (based on the OPM). Over the next 38 years, the elderly poverty rate fell further to 9.1 percent in 2012. The deceleration in poverty reduction is less pronounced for nonelderly adults and children. In fact, using the SPM measure that accounts for expansions of the EITC and non-cash transfers, children's poverty had greater declines in the 1990s than in the 1960s or 1970s.

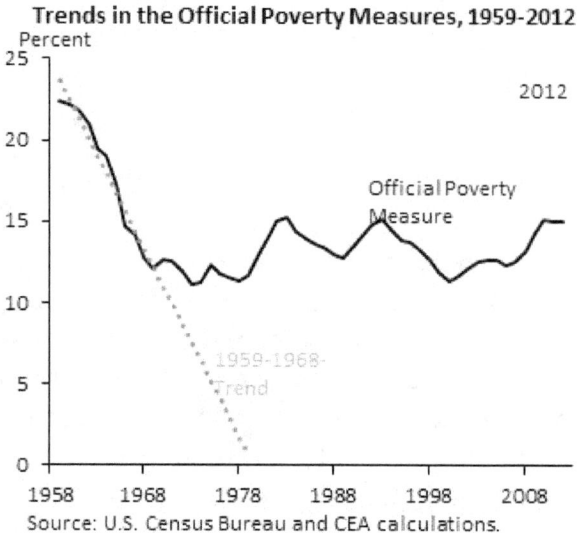

Figure 1

Trends in the Official Poverty Measures, 1959-2012

Percent

Source: U.S. Census Bureau and CEA calculations.

Growth in inequality also helped put the brakes on improvements in cash income for most households. Economic growth is an important determinant of poverty (Blank 2000) as long as the gains are shared with those in the bottom of the income distribution. When growth fails to benefit the bottom, it cannot play a role in eradicating poverty. As such, the distribution of income can have a profound impact on the level of poverty. While the real economy grew at an annual rate of about 2.1 percent during the 1970s and 1980s, since 1980 economic growth has not produced the "rising tide" heralded by President Kennedy, as rising inequality left incomes at the bottom relatively unchanged (DiNardo, Fortin, Lemieux 1996, Piketty and Saez 2003, Lemieux 2008). As shown in Figure 2, incomes in the top quintile of the income distribution rose dramatically until the 2000s and are about 50 percent higher today than in 1973. By contrast, real household incomes in the bottom 60 percent of the income distribution stagnated until the mid-1990s expansion, and today are little changed from the business cycle peak in 1973.

Figure 2

Average Real Household Income by Quintile, 1967-2012

Index (1973=100)

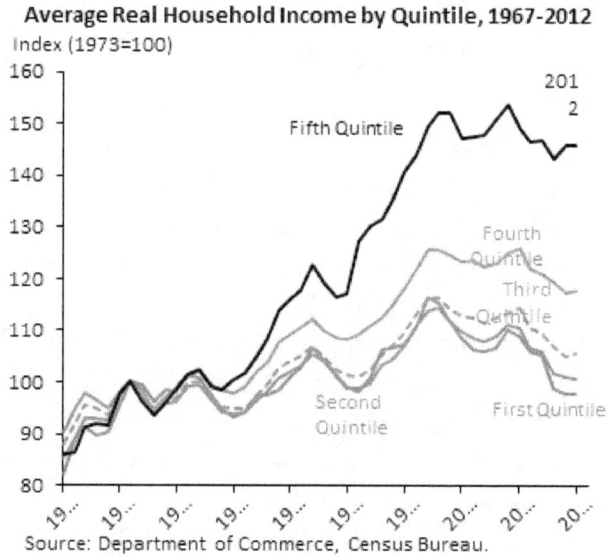

Source: Department of Commerce, Census Bureau.

A large group of poverty scholars have pointed to this rise in inequality as a leading explanation for the lack of progress in reducing poverty since 1980 (for example, Blank 1993, Gottschalk and Danziger 1995 and 2003, Hoynes et al. 2006).

The failure of the minimum wage to keep up with inflation is an important reason why inequality increased in the 1980s (DiNardo, Fortin, and Lemieux 1996, Lee 1999), and progress in the fight against poverty has slowed. President Johnson extended both the level and scope of the minimum wage, with its peak reached in real terms in 1968. Since then the minimum wage has risen and fallen, but today its level of $7.25 an hour is the same in real terms as in 1950. At this level, even factoring in the subsidy provided by the EITC, a single parent of two kids working full time would still have income near the poverty line.

Several studies have documented a tight link between the value of the minimum wage and measures of wage inequality in the bottom part of the income distribution (Lee 1999, DiNardo, Fortin, and Lemieux 1996). For example, as shown in Figure 3, changes in the ratio of the median wage to the 10th percentile of the wage distribution (the "50-10 wage gap")—a measure of inequality in the bottom of the wage distribution—for women correlate very closely with changes in the real value of the minimum wage.[11] The best research suggests that increases in the minimum wage do not result in job losses large enough to undermine the goal of raising incomes for the poor (Dube, Lester, Reich 2010). Moreover, a recent meta-analysis by Doucouliagos and Stanley (2009) covering over 1,000 estimates of minimum wage effects finds "no evidence of a meaningful adverse employment effect." Finally, a recent analysis and review of the literature by Dube (2014) finds consistent evidence across studies that a 10 percent increase in the minimum wage decreases the poverty rate by about 2.4 percent.

Another important factor in rising inequality and slow wage growth among low- and middle-income workers has been the decline in unionization. The percent of U.S. workers represented by unions has nearly halved from 23.5 percent in 1983 to 12.5 percent in 2012.[12] This decline has contributed to inequality because unions reduce inequality by raising the wages of low- and middle-income workers and compressing the returns to skill (DiNardo et al. 1996, DiNardo and Lemieux 1997).

Many observers have implicated various demographic changes—most prominently, increased immigration and a decline in two-parent families—as additional factors behind the lack of progress in market incomes in the lower part of the distribution. The recent literature on immigration rejects the claim that competition from immigrants has had a meaningfully adverse effect on the wages or poverty rates of native workers (Peri 2013). Because the country-of-origin composition of immigrants has increasingly shifted towards poorer countries, however, immigration has had a mechanical effect on poverty rates. Card and Raphael (2013) estimate that changes in the population shares and the country of origin of the foreign born increased overall poverty rates (based on OPM) by 3.7 percentage points between 1970 and 2009. While some immigrant households that may have seen their incomes rise as a result of coming to the United States, many still fall below the poverty line here. But other analysts focusing on different time periods generally find much smaller compositional effects. For example, Hoynes et al. (2006) find that increased immigration accounts for only a 0.1 percentage point increase in poverty between 1979 and 1999.

Another dramatic change that has occurred since the 1960s is a large increase in the number of people living in single-female headed households. As shown in Table 1, individuals in such households typically have double the poverty rates of the national average, so this change also tends to increase the poverty rate. Using decomposition techniques, Hoynes et al. (2006) show that changes in family structure alone accounted for a 3.7 percentage point increase in the (OPM) poverty rate between 1967 and 2003.[13] In fact, women's poverty rates declined over this time period, however, since their educational attainment, labor force participation, and earnings increased and they had fewer children, all of which reduced their poverty rates (Reed and Cancian 2001). Moreover, changes in family structure can both cause and be caused by changes in economic circumstances.

The last three decades have also seen a historic rise in incarceration, which has led to greater poverty. The fraction of the population in prison rose from 221 per 100,000 in 1980 to 762 per 100,000 in 2008 (Western and Pettit 2010).[14] In the short term, imprisonment removes wage

---

[12] Retrieved from http://data.bls.gov/cgi-bin/surveymost?lu, December 10, 2013.

[13] Like all decompositions, the reference period matters. If the decomposition is performed using 2009 poverty rates rather than those in 1970, the predicted increase is 2.8 percentage points.

[14] Research suggests the increase is driven primarily by increased sentencing severity rather than increases in criminal activity (Caplow and Simon 1999, Nicholson-Crotty and Meier 2003).

earners from the family, which reduces their family's income and increases the probability of their children growing up in poverty. For example, Johnson (2008) finds that child poverty increases by 8.5 percentage points and family income falls by an average of $8,800 while a father is in prison.

There are also long-term negative impacts on earnings from incarceration that lead to higher rates of poverty among those with a criminal record. Offenders' wages are lower by between 3 and 16 percent after incarceration (Raphael 2007; Western 2002) and employment and labor force participation are also negatively affected. Research shows that each additional percentage point of imprisonment of African American men is associated with a reduction in employment or labor force participation of young African American men of approximately 1.0 to 1.5 percentage points. This relationship implies that the increases in incarceration over the last three decades have reduced employment and labor force participation among young African American males by 3 to 5 percentage points (Holzer 2007). Holzer also notes that while the magnitude of the effect of incarceration on White and Latino offenders is less clear, most studies find that their experience with employment and labor force participation after incarceration is similar to that of African American men.

Together the factors described above created headwinds in the fight on poverty. Evaluating the precise impact of these factors is beyond the scope of this report, but it is likely that their combined influence was to exert modest upward pressure on poverty rates. As we shall see below, the fact that "market poverty" stayed relatively constant over this time period suggests that improvements in education or other factors may have offset the adverse effects of these demographic and other changes. Previous studies based on the OPM support this notion. For example, Mishel et al. (2013) suggest that the impact of increases in education in reducing poverty were slightly greater than the adverse impact of changing demographics.

Correcting the Historical Account of Poverty Since the 1960s

The official poverty measure introduced by President Johnson's administration ignores, by design, the most important antipoverty programs introduced during and after the War on Poverty. In particular, resources from nutrition assistance, tax credits for working families, and access to health insurance are not considered when computing whether a family is poor by the traditional metric.

The Census Bureau has published the Supplemental Poverty Measure only as far back as 2009. But recent research by poverty scholars on alternate measures of poverty all find that the official poverty rate displayed in Figure 1 dramatically understates the decline in poverty since the 1960s (Fox et al. 2013, U.S. Census Bureau 2013, Meyer and Sullivan 2013, Sherman 2013). Work by Wimer, Fox, Garfinkel, Kaushal, and Waldfogel (2013) is particularly valuable since they estimate poverty rates from 1967 to 2012 following the SPM methodology for computing family resources. They also measure poverty using an "anchored" measure that uses a fixed poverty threshold based on expenditures on necessary items in 2012, adjusted only for inflation in each year (with inflation measured using a historically consistent series, the CPI-U-RS).[15]

Figure 4 shows a striking fact: poverty has declined by 38 percent since 1967, according to the anchored SPM measure. And, unlike the OPM, it continued to fall after the early 1970s. The figure shows the evolution of the poverty rate using the anchored SPM measure of poverty from 1967 to 2012, compared with the official poverty rate reproduced from Figure 1. Using the more accurate SPM measure of family resources changes the historical account of poverty in the United States significantly: between 1967 and 2012, poverty rates fell by 9.8 percentage points—from 25.8 to 16.0 percent. The trend in the SPM depicted in Figure 4 is very similar to that of an alternative measure of poverty based on consumption data, which Meyer and Sullivan (2013) argue is a better measure of material hardship (see box).

Figure 4 shows that the fraction of Americans in poverty fell smoothly between 1967 and 1979 to a low of 17.4 percent, a period where the discrepancy with the trend shown by the official measure is driven primarily by more accurate accounting for inflation in the 1970s. After rising steeply during the double-dip recession of the early 1980s, poverty rates fell slightly until rising again with the early 1990s recession.

---

[15] The 'anchored poverty' measure allows progress to be measured against a constant definition of living standards. Using the SPM methodology of updating poverty thresholds each year to reflect rising expenditures on food, clothing, shelter, and utilities shows less of a decline in poverty since the real value of the poverty thresholds rise over time (Fox et al. 2013). Data constraints prevent Wimer et al. (2013) from following the SPM methodology exactly. The most important discrepancy from the Census procedure is that Wimer et al. do not adjust the poverty thresholds for geographic differences in living costs. It is worth noting that an alternative measure anchors poverty thresholds based on necessary expenditures in 1967, and adjusts for inflation each year afterwards. Both measures show similar declines in poverty, but using expenditures in 2012 gives a higher level of poverty in every period since increased real spending on necessities over time has led to a higher SPM poverty threshold.

Consumption-based poverty measures the amount households spend relative to a threshold on goods and services, and estimated "service flows" from large, infrequent purchases like housing and automobiles. Meyer and Sullivan argue in a series of papers (2003, 2012a, 2012b, 2013) that consumption provides a better measure of resources for low-income households since it reflects accumulated assets, expected future income, access to credit, assistance from family and friends, non-market income, and the insurance value of government programs. They also argue that consumption data are more accurately reported relative to some safety net benefits included in the SPM, especially for households in or near poverty.

The figure shows the trend in Meyer and Sullivan's (2013) measure of consumption poverty, updated through 2012 and normalized to have the same level as the SPM measure in 2012. Although the underlying methodologies differ, the trends in consumption poverty and SPM income poverty have been remarkably similar over time. For example, the declines in poverty between 1972 and 2012 shown by each measure are nearly identical.

It is difficult to identify the effects of particular government programs on consumption poverty because one cannot easily identify and remove the consumption derived from particular government programs as one can with income under the SPM. However, the fact that the two measures are similar suggests that underreporting of benefits has little impact at the margin of determining whether someone is poor. Additionally, the similarities in the measure suggest that spending through savings or borrowing from friends and family is rarely able to keep someone out of poverty.

In contrast to the depiction of the OPM, the steepest declines in the fraction of people in poverty occurred during the economic expansion of the 1990s. During that period, poverty fell from 21.5 percent in 1993 to 15.3 percent in 2000, the lowest poverty rate observed since 1967. As shown in Figure 2, economic growth in the 1990s provided a strong boost to low-income households as earnings grew even in the bottom quintile of incomes, in contrast to the experience of any other decade since the 1960s. Dramatic increases in the value of the EITC leveraged this upswing in the labor market to further encourage work and channel even more resources to low-income working families.

One last, and remarkable, fact shown in Figure 4 is that the poverty rate ticked up only slightly during the Great Recession after remaining steady for most of the 2000s. Despite the largest rise in unemployment since the Great Depression, the poverty rates rose by only 0.5 percentage points overall between 2007 and 2010. As discussed below, this shows how effective the safety net and its expansion through the 2009 American Recovery and Reinvestment Act (the Recovery Act) have been. Since much of the credit for this is due to expansions in SNAP and tax credits, the official poverty rate fails to capture this crucial success.

The poverty rates for children and for working-age adults follow a similar pattern to the overall trend shown in Figure 4. The fraction of children living in poverty declined from 29.4 percent in 1967 to 18.7 percent in 2012; and for working-age adults, the poverty rate fell from 19.8 to 15.1 percent over the same period. For the elderly, the trend in poverty is one of near continuous decline. Poverty fell quite rapidly up until the early 1980s, driven by large growth in per capita Social Security payments, from 46.5 percent in 1967 to 20.7 percent in 1984. Elderly poverty fell further during the 1990s expansion to a low of 16.5 percent in 1999, and then ticked up slightly in the 2000s. Driven in part by the Recovery Act stimulus payments, elderly poverty declined from 17.6 percent to 15.2 percent between 2007 and 2009, and it remains at that level in 2012.

Measuring the Direct Impact of Antipoverty Efforts

The fact that poverty rates have fallen overall, even as household incomes in the bottom of the distribution have stagnated since the 1980s, suggests a substantial direct role that policies have played in improving the well-being of the poor. Wimer et al. (2013) estimate the magnitude of this impact by constructing "counterfactual" poverty measures that simulate the fraction of the population that would have been poor in the absence of all government transfers, including the overall tax system. [16] In other words, they estimate the fraction of families that would have incomes below the poverty line if the value of all cash, in-kind, and tax transfers they received (or paid if the family owed taxes on net) were not counted. Comparing the difference between this measure of "market poverty" and the SPM poverty rate provides a measure of the reduction in poverty accounted for by government transfers. Figure 5 shows the results of this

---

[16] While this is a 'static' exercise in that it assumes that individual earnings themselves are not affected by the existence of safety net programs, this report later reviews research on the effects of programs on employment and earnings and finds that such effects are generally small where they exist, and not large enough to meaningfully alter the conclusions from this simplification (Ben-Shalom, Moffitt, and Scholz 2010).

analysis. The height of the overall shaded region indicates the poverty rate counting only market income, while the height of the region shaded in black is the SPM poverty rate shown in Figure 4. The difference, shaded in green, represents the percentage of the population lifted from poverty by the safety net and the net effect of the tax system.[17]

Figure 5

In part because of the rising inequality in earnings described above, market poverty *increased* over the past 45 years by 1.7 percentage points from 27.0 percent in 1967 to 28.7 percent in 2012. In contrast, poverty rates that are measured including taxes and transfers—these taxes and transfers are the green shaded region in the Figure—fell through most of this period. Government transfers reduced poverty by 1.2 percentage points in 1967. This impact grew to about 7.4 percentage points by 1975 due to the expansion of the safety net spurred by the War on Poverty, and hovered around that level until the Great Recession when it increased to 12.7 percentage points in 2012.

Despite an increase in "market poverty" of 4.5 percentage points between 2007 and 2010, the actual SPM poverty rate rose only 0.5 percentage points due to the safety net. In fact, the 2009 Recovery Act reduced poverty by 1.8 percentage points in 2010 through its extensions to the safety net as discussed below. Overall, for the entire 45-year period, the poverty decline of 9.8

---

[17] There are two counterfactuals estimated by Wimer et al. that are used in this report to discuss the impact of the safety net. For most estimates of the impact of the safety net we use a counterfactual poverty rate that strips away ("zeroes out") all cash and in-kind transfers, as well as refundable tax credits but continues to subtract any "normal" tax liability from family resources. In this section, we define "market poverty" similarly, only this measure additionally zeroes out all tax liabilities. Since poor families near the poverty line tend to have positive tax liabilities, market poverty rates are slightly—about 1.8 percentage points in 2012—lower (since we assume families can keep the taxes they in fact must pay).

percentage points is almost entirely accounted for by the increased effectiveness of the safety net.[18]

Figure 6 shows a similar analysis of the effect of the safety net on trends in deep poverty and highlights two important features of the safety net often overlooked. First, the safety net improves the well-being of many more individuals than is reflected in the standard accounting of how many individuals are lifted from poverty: in 2012, about one in twenty (5.3 percent) Americans lived in deep poverty, yet without government transfers the number would be closer to one in five (18.8 percent).

Second, the safety net almost entirely eliminates cyclical swings in the prevalence of deep poverty. Figure 6 shows that despite large increases in deep market poverty driven by the business cycle, there is little if any rise in actual deep poverty due to the supports provided by the safety net.

Figure 6

Again, this phenomenon is especially visible during the Great Recession, when the prevalence of deep poverty ticked upward by only 0.2 percentage points despite an increase in market deep poverty of 3.3 percentage points. This corresponds to more than 9.6 million men, women, and children prevented from living below one-half the poverty line during the Great Recession. Over the 45 years shown in the Figure, deep "market poverty" actually rises from 14.9 to 18.8 percent. Despite that increase, the fraction of those in deep poverty fell from 8.2 to 5.3 percent.

---

[18] As described earlier, the underreporting of government income and benefits means that this is likely to be a conservative lower-bound estimate of the effect of the safety net.

While women continue to have a higher poverty rate than men, the gap has decreased over time as poverty has fallen more for women than for men. The following chart shows that the gap between working-age women and men has decreased from 4.7 percent to 1.7 percent from 1967 to 2012.

The decline in the poverty rate among women has been tempered by an increase in the number of single mothers, who have higher rates of poverty. The share of working age women who are single mothers rose from 11.6 to 16.1 percent between 1967 and 2012. Had the poverty rates of demographic groups (based on marriage and motherhood only) remained as they were in 1967, this change would have increased poverty rates for working age women by 2.1 percentage points. In fact, poverty rates of women in all marriage and motherhood groups fell due to increased work, rising education, and smaller families (Cancian and Reed 2009), as well as to the increased impact of the safety net described in this report.

The effect of government transfer and social insurance programs on poverty is slightly larger for women than for men. These programs reduced the 2012 poverty rate by 8.1 percentage points for women compared to 6.4 percentage points for men. This gender difference has been fairly stable over time, indicating that growth in these programs does not explain the narrowing poverty gap shown above. Rather, the closing of the gender poverty gap appears to be due to increases in women's education and employment rates relative to men.

III.   The Role of Antipoverty Programs: A Closer Look

"Poverty ... has many faces. ... its roots are many and its causes complex. To defeat it requires a coordinated and comprehensive attack. No single program can embrace all who are poor, and no single program can strike at all the sources of today's and tomorrow's poverty."

— 1964 Economic Report of the President.

This section presents further detail on antipoverty effects of specific components of the safety net. In particular, it highlights the impact that different groups of programs—cash transfers, in-kind transfers, and tax credits—have on the poverty rates of different age groups. It also shows how the relative importance of programs for nonelderly adults and children has changed since the start of the War on Poverty.

The section then refutes the concern critics have raised that the existence of safety net programs may undermine growth in market incomes as well as our efforts to fight poverty. The social safety net has increasingly been designed to reward and facilitate work increasing participation rates—in many cases, requiring work. Even where programs are not explicitly designed to require work, the highest-quality studies suggest that adverse earnings effects of safety net programs are nonexistent or very small, in part due to reforms over the past two decades that, for example, have phased out benefits gradually with increases in earnings to minimize disincentives to work.

Finally, this section presents findings on the level of economic mobility of individuals born into poverty in the United States, and the results of recent research showing the potentially large returns to social spending in terms of long-term outcomes of children in families receiving support.

Antipoverty Effects of Specific Programs

This section illustrates the role that various antipoverty programs have had in improving the well-being of different populations, and how the relative impacts of these programs have evolved since the War on Poverty began. It is based on an effectively "static" analysis that zeroes out income derived from various public programs to ask what effect this would have on poverty. The next subsection considers some of the broader impacts that these programs have on employment and earnings.

Table 2 shows the impact of various safety net programs on overall poverty, and for three separate age groups: children, adults age 19 to 64, and elderly adults age 65 and over. The safety net program with the single greatest impact is Social Security, which provides income to the elderly, people with disabilities, and surviving spouses and children, reducing the overall poverty rate by 8.5 percentage points in 2012. The program's impacts on elderly poverty are profound: without Social Security income, the poverty rate of the elderly would be 54.7 percent, rather than its rate of 14.8 percent in 2012. On the other end of the age spectrum, refundable tax credits like the Earned

Table 2

Poverty Rate Reduction from Government Programs, 2012

	All People	Children	Nonelderly Adults	65 Years and Older
Social Security	8.56	1.97	4.08	39.86
Refundable Tax Credits	3.02	6.66	2.25	0.20
SNAP	1.62	3.01	1.27	0.76
Unemployment Insurance	0.79	0.82	0.88	0.31
SSI	1.07	0.84	1.12	1.21
Housing subsidies	0.91	1.39	0.66	1.12
School lunch	0.38	0.91	0.25	0.03
TANF/General Assistance	0.21	0.46	0.14	0.05
WIC	0.13	0.29	0.09	0.00
Population (Thousands)	311,116	74,046	193,514	43,245

Note: Data are presented as percentage points.

Source: Department of Commerce, Census Bureau.

Income Tax Credit and the Child Tax Credit have large impacts on child poverty— reducing the fraction of children in poverty by 6.7 percentage points. Tax credits also reduce the poverty rates of nonelderly adults by 2.3 percentage points. The Supplemental Nutrition Assistance Program also has a dramatic effect on poverty, reducing child poverty by 3.0 percentage points and overall poverty rates by 1.6 percentage points.

Finally, unemployment insurance reduced poverty by 0.8 percent overall in 2012. This effect, as with the effects for other programs, was less than at the height of the Great Recession when more people were without work: in 2010, for example, unemployment insurance reduced poverty by 1.5 percentage points overall (Short 2012).

As noted, all of these estimates ignore the incentives to alter work behavior created by government programs and are not definitive causal estimates of the impact of the different programs on poverty. For example, Social Security may affect market incomes by changing retirement and savings incentives. Similarly, the estimates do not take into account the role that UI plays in keeping people attached to the labor force, or that the EITC plays in incentivizing additional hours of work and participation in the labor force. The importance of these considerations is discussed below.

Even programs with a small impact on overall poverty rates may be very effective in reducing poverty for certain populations or in alleviating hardship without lifting individuals out of poverty. For example, SSI reduces poverty rates by 1.1 percentage point overall, but this represents a large poverty reduction concentrated among a relatively small number of low-income recipients who are elderly or have a disability. TANF and General Assistance (state programs which typically provide limited aid to very poor individuals not qualifying for other aid) have only a small impact on the overall poverty rate at 0.2 percentage points, as TANF benefits are generally insufficient to bring people above the poverty level. However, by raising the incomes of those in poverty these programs have a much greater impact on reducing deep poverty.

Based on their historical estimates of SPM poverty rates, Wimer et al. (2013) conduct similar analyses to those in Table 2 for each year since 1967 for different groups of safety net programs. Their results shed light on how the safety net has changed over the past 50 years.

In aggregate, the antipoverty effects of three types of federal aid programs—support through cash programs like Social Security, SSI, and TANF; in-kind support like SNAP and housing assistance; and tax credits like the EITC and CTC—all increase over time, driving down overall poverty rates. The steady increase in the effect of each type of program masks some differences across the populations served by each program. For the elderly, for example, the trend is dominated by the growing real value of Social Security payments steadily driving down the elderly poverty rate.

SOCIAL PROGRAMS SERVE ALL AMERICANS

While the safety net provides crucial support for families in poverty, far more Americans benefit from the safety net than are poor in any given year. Of course, all Americans benefit from Social Security and Medicare support for the aged, shielding both them and their families from low income in retirement and the costs of adverse health shocks. And many people benefit from social insurance programs that are not means-tested. For example, nearly half of all Americans will benefit from unemployment insurance at some point over a 20-year period.

But even programs targeting primarily low- income families serve a very high fraction of Americans at some point in their lives. A recent studying using administrative tax records from 1989 to 2006 found that over 50 percent of tax -filers with children benefited from the EITC at some point over the 19 year period (Dowd and Horowitz 2011). Moreover, CEA analysis of the National Longitudinal Study of Youth 1979 finds that of all individuals aged 14 to 22 in 1979, over the 32-year period from 1978 to 2010:
  ➢ 29.6 percent benefitted from SNAP;
  ➢ 34.3 percent received support from SNAP, AFDC/TANF, or SSI; and
  ➢ 69.2 percent received income from SNAP, AFDC/TANF, SSI, or UI.

Looking at a broader array of programs, a large fraction of the population benefits in any given year as well. According to the 2013 Annual Demographic and Economic Supplement of the Current Population Survey, nearly half (47.5 percent) of all households received support from either refundable tax credits, SNAP, Unemployment Insurance, SSI, housing assistance, school lunch, TANF, WIC, Medicaid or Disability Insurance.

An important feature of the safety net that is often overlooked: for most programs the majority of beneficiaries receive assistance for only a short period when their earnings drop for some reason, and then they bounce out again. Research has shown, for example, that 61 percent of all EITC recipients claimed the credit for two years or less (Dowd and Horowitz 2011); and, half of all new SNAP participants in the mid-2000s left the program within 10 months.

For children, however, there is a shift in importance of the safety net's different components. Figure 7 shows the effect of eliminating various components of the safety net resources on the SPM poverty rate in three years corresponding to recession-driven peaks of the poverty rate. In the early 1970s recession, AFDC, and food stamps to a lesser extent, played the most important role in alleviating childhood poverty; and the EITC had not yet been introduced. Both in-kind transfers and the EITC had a small impact on child poverty in the early 1990s recession, but cash transfer programs still outweighed the poverty-reducing impact of both programs put together. During the Great Recession, however, we see that in-kind aid, cash-assistance, and tax credits all played similarly important roles in reducing poverty for families with children. This shift reflects both the large structural change away from cash welfare assistance during the 1990s, and expansion of both SNAP and tax credits through the Recovery Act.

Figure 8 is similar to Figure 7, only showing the impact of various transfer programs on deep poverty, or the fraction of individuals with incomes below 50 percent of the poverty threshold. This figure shows that for deep poverty, in-kind transfers have become the most important safety net program over time, and tax credits are less effective due to the paucity of work among families with very low resources.

The Effects of Antipoverty Programs on Work and Earnings

In his remarks before signing the cornerstone legislation of the War on Poverty, the Economic Opportunity Act, President Johnson declared: "Our American answer to poverty is not to make the poor more secure in their poverty but to reach down and to help them lift themselves out of the ruts of poverty and move with the large majority along the high road of hope and prosperity. The days of the dole in our country are numbered." He went on to describe the need to provide the poor with the means to lift themselves out of poverty through job training and employment services, among other strategies. In the past 20 years, this emphasis on promoting work through antipoverty programs intensified and we made dramatic changes to cash welfare and other programs that shifted the focus toward requiring or rewarding work.

The most important shift began when President Richard Nixon introduced the Earned Income Tax Credit in 1975. The EITC was expanded multiple times in the 1980s, 1990s, and 2000s as the safety net shifted increasingly toward work-based support. The EITC was expanded most recently in the 2009 Recovery Act, with those improvements extended in 2010 and 2013. Since 1996, the EITC has accounted for more support for low-income households than traditional cash welfare. Today, the EITC and the partially refundable Child Tax Credit total $77 billion annually, nearly four times as the expenditures on the Temporary Assistance for Needy Families program (see Figure 9).

Because the EITC is a supplement to labor market earnings, the credit provides strong incentives for those with otherwise low labor force attachment to increase their hours of work. However, because the credit is reduced as earnings continue to rise, it may also provide those with earnings above the phase-out threshold—above $22,870 for a married couple with three children—an incentive to reduce their earnings. Several studies have addressed these incentive effects, and reach similar conclusions: the EITC is associated with increased labor force participation, especially among single mothers, but it does not appear to substantially alter the hours or earnings of those already working (Eissa and Liebman 1996, Liebman 1998, Meyer and Rosenbaum 2001, Hotz and Scholz 2003, and Eissa and Hoynes 2005).[19] Taken together, these results suggest EITC expansions played an important role in increasing labor force participation among single mothers, without adversely affecting hours worked by those already working.

Meanwhile, the 1996 welfare reform law replaced AFDC with TANF and significantly strengthened work requirements in the cash assistance program. The Personal Responsibility and Work Opportunity Reconciliation Act of 1996 ended the entitlement to cash assistance and beneficiaries were generally required to work or participate in "work activities" to receive assistance. Moreover, the implicit tax rate on benefits in response to increased earnings—the

---

[19] For example, Meyer and Rosenbaum (2001) suggest that EITC expansion accounts for about 60 percent of the roughly 10 percentage point rise in single mothers' employment rates relative to single mothers without children between 1984 and 1996.

benefit reduction rate—was reduced dramatically in many states. Matsudaira and Blank (2013) show that these changes increased the return to work, with potential income gains of over $1,842 (in 2000 dollars) for welfare recipients working 30 hours a week. At the same time, it should be noted that researchers have found these reforms may have increased hardship among groups with high barriers to employment, highlighting the continued importance of programs that serve the most disadvantaged (Blank 2007; Turner, Danziger, and Seefeldt 2006).

While today's safety net has been reformed to promote work, it is important to note that careful research has shown that most assistance programs have only small, if any, disincentive effects on work. This suggests that the "static" estimates of the antipoverty effects of the programs shown above largely capture the actual full impact of these programs including any employment disincentives they may have—and may understate the poverty-reducing impacts of programs that effectively reward and facilitate work and thus increase market earnings. For example, examining labor supply behavior of individuals in the Oregon Health Insurance Experiment, Baicker et al. (2013) find that Medicaid recipients are not less likely to be employed nor do they earn less than they otherwise would have. Similarly, Hoynes and Schanzenbach (2007) study the initial rollout of SNAP (then food stamps) and find only small effects on labor supply. While there are no studies of the employment effects of the TANF program with its work requirements, prior studies of AFDC and the Negative Income Tax experiments of the 1970's suggest only modest disincentive effects of a program without an emphasis on work. Burtless (1986) found that a dollar of benefits reduces work earnings by 20 cents (total income is increased by 80 cents), but other evidence suggests the disincentive effects may have been even smaller (SRI International 1983).

Evaluating the weight of the evidence for all programs, Ben-Shalom, Moffitt, and Sholz (2012) conclude that the work disincentive effects of antipoverty programs have "basically, zero" effect on overall poverty rates. Going program by program, they conclude the behavioral effects of TANF are likely zero, and that the work disincentives induced by disability insurance, Medicare, and Unemployment Insurance might reduce the estimated "static" antipoverty effects of those programs by one-eighth or less. Although housing assistance provides significant benefits to some of the poorest households including the homeless, its effects on labor supply among those of working age and free of disabilities are relatively modest. Shroder (2010) reports that the net negative impact of rental assistance on labor supply appears to vary among subgroups, may change over time, and seems rather small relative to the amounts paid out in subsidy. Jacob and Ludwig (2012) find that receipt of housing vouchers in Chicago during the welfare reform era reduced employment by 3.6 percentage points among able-bodied working-age individuals and reduced earnings an average 19 cents for each dollar of subsidies. Carlson et al. (2011) find employment effects in the same range for Wisconsin voucher recipients. Ben-Shalom et al. estimate that the poverty rate among housing assistance recipients is 66.0 percent, and use the Jacob and Ludwig data to estimate that housing assistance lowers the poverty rate among recipients by 8.2 percentage points rather than the static estimate of 14.9 points. Finally, a recent study by Chetty, Friedman, and Saez (2012) of the EITC on the earnings distribution also finds that "the impacts of the EITC ... come primarily through its mechanical effects." They do find, however, that behavioral responses reinforce the amplify the effects of the safety net on deep poverty, so that the overall impact of the EITC might be somewhat greater than implied by the "static" estimates because of the increased work induced by the program.[20]

Economic Mobility

When economic mobility is high, individuals and families can lift themselves out of poverty by taking advantage of opportunities to improve their economic well-being. When economic mobility is low, it is difficult to change one's economic status and people may become stuck in poverty. Mobility can be measured either as relative mobility—the likelihood of moving up or down the income distribution—or absolute mobility, which is the likelihood of improving economic well-being in general without necessarily moving up in the income distribution (reflected in the saying, "a rising tide lifts all boats"). When there is low relative mobility, there are few opportunities for poor people to improve their standing in society by moving up the economic spectrum, and children from poor families are likely to continue to have low economic and social status as they become adults, even if their material well-being improves. When there is low absolute mobility, poor people and their children find it hard to escape the economic and material hardships of poverty.

While economic mobility in the United States allows some people to escape poverty, many do not. About half of the poorest individuals remain in the lowest fifth of the income distribution after 10 and 20 years, and no more than one-fourth make it to one of the top three income quintiles (Acs and Zimmerman 2008; Auten et al. 2013). Those who were in poor families as children are estimated to have 20 to 40 percent lower earnings as adults compared to those who did not grow up in poverty (Mayer 1997; Corcoran and Adams 1997; Corcoran 2001; Duncan et al. 2012). Among the children of low-earning fathers, about two-fifths of sons and one-fourth of daughters remained in the lowest earnings quintile when they became their father's age (Jantti et al. 2006). Consistent with this, one-third of children who grew up in the lowest family income quintile were in the lowest quintile when they became adults (Isaacs 2008). More generally, studies find that about one-third to slightly less than one-half of parents' incomes are reflected in their children's incomes later in life (Chetty et al. 2013, Black and Devereux 2011, Lee and Solon 2009), indicating that parents heavily influence children's economic fortunes.

The results of these studies imply strong lingering effects from growing up in poverty. The influence of poverty on future economic prospects stem not just from one's own family status, but from growing up in high-poverty neighborhoods that often have lower-quality schools, lower-paying jobs, higher crime rates, and other conditions that can create disadvantages (Sharkey 2009). Among children whose families were in the top three quintiles of family income, growing up in a high-poverty neighborhood raises the likelihood of downward mobility

---

[20] Unlike the earlier literature, they also find evidence of a slight downward adjustment of earnings for workers near 200 percent of the poverty line. This is consistent with the predictions of static labor supply theory since that level of earnings is in the phase-out region of the credit. This negative impact is small, however, and Chetty et al. emphasize it is dominated by the (also small) positive impacts at low earnings levels.

(falling at least one quintile) by 52 percent (Sharkey 2009). A comparison across geographic regions in the United States indicates that economic mobility is higher in areas with a larger middle class, less residential segregation between low-income and middle-income individuals, higher social capital, and lower rates of teen birth, crime, divorce, and children raised by single parents (Chetty et al. 2013).

The above results mostly reflect relative mobility (moving up or down the economic spectrum). While absolute mobility (improving economic well-being without moving up the economic spectrum) has generally risen in the United States, the pace has slowed in recent decades. Comparing cohorts of men in their 30's, median personal income went up 5 percent from 1964 to 1994, but down 12 percent from 1974 to 2004 (Sawhill and Morton 2007). Counting all family income, income went up 32 percent between 1964 and 1994, and only 9 percent between 1974 and 2004. So the recent improvement in family income, which reflects the rising employment of women, was only one-third as large as in the earlier period.[21]

Despite the popular view that the United States is the land of opportunity, this Nation appears to have lower economic mobility than many other developed countries. Measuring mobility by the strength of the dependence of children's incomes on parents' incomes, the United States has similar mobility as the United Kingdom and Italy, but lower mobility than other European countries as well as with Japan, Australia, and Canada (Solon 2002; Jantti et al. 2006; Corak 2006, 2011).

Can anything be done to increase mobility? A study of data on families over time (including comparisons of twins and other siblings) found that genetics and shared upbringing play a significant, but overall minor role, in explaining adult earnings differences, indicating that environmental factors other than upbringing are largely responsible (Bjorklund et al. 2005).

Education appears to be one of the key factors that drives economic mobility. As shown in Figure 10, among families in the bottom fifth of the income distribution, almost half (45 percent) of the children who did not obtain college degrees remained in the poorest fifth as adults, while only one-sixth (16 percent) of the children who obtained college degrees remained in the poorest fifth (Isaacs, Sawhill, and Haskins 2008: 95).

---

[21] Using a different method to assess absolute mobility, about half of individuals moved out of the bottom income quintile in the 1984-94 and 1994-2004 periods when the quintile thresholds were fixed at the beginning of the period (Acs and Zimmerman, 2008).

The importance of education is also shown by the findings that economic mobility is higher in countries that have a greater public expenditure on education (Ichino et al. 2009) and areas of the United States that have a higher-quality K-12 education system (Chetty et al. 2013), and is improved for children in the poorest one-third of families when states increase spending on elementary and secondary education (Mayer and Lopoo 2008).

Intergenerational Returns

While much of the literature on mobility presented above is correlational, a handful of well-crafted studies that track the long-run outcomes of children exposed to safety net programs highlight the potential for investments in these programs to generate large returns.

Early childhood education has been found by many researchers to have dramatic, super-normal returns in terms of more favorable adult outcomes. The Head Start program created early in the War on Poverty has been heavily researched and the combined results show that it can "rightfully be considered a success for much of the past fifty years" (Gibbs et al. 2013: 61). Studies following children over time, and accounting for the influence of family background by comparing siblings, found that Head Start participants were more likely to complete high school and attend college (Garces et al. 2002), and scored higher on a summary index of young adult outcomes that also included crime, teen parenthood, health status, and idleness (Deming 2009). The latter study found that Head Start closed one-third of the gap in the summary outcome index between children in families at the median and bottom quartiles of family income. Using a regression discontinuity research design that compared access to Head Start across counties, Ludwig and Miller (2007) found positive impacts of Head Start on schooling attainment, the likelihood of attending college, and mortality rates from causes that could be affected by Head Start. Gibbs et al. (2013) suggest the combination of the benefits due to Head Start might produce a benefit-cost ratio in excess of seven.

Randomized experiments studying the Perry Preschool Project, Abecedarian Project, Chicago Child-Parent Centers, Early Training Project, and Project CARE programs largely confirm these findings. A variety of well-done analyses find that the adult benefits for children—especially girls—who participated included higher educational attainment, employment, and earnings along with other benefits (Schweinhart et al. 2005; Anderson 2008; Campbell et al. 2008; Heckman et al. 2007, 2010, 2011). Heckman and coauthors (2009) find that the returns to one preschool program (Perry) exceed the returns to equities.

In the past decade, researchers have identified long-run linkages between early childhood (including exposure in-utero) health interventions and long-term outcomes. For example, Almond, Chay, and Greenstone (2006) document that the Johnson administration used the threat of withheld federal funds for the newly introduced Medicare program to force hospitals to comply with the Civil Rights Act mandate to desegregate, resulting in dramatic improvements in infant health and large declines in the black-white gap in infant mortality in the 1960s. Chay, Guryan, and Mazumder (2009) show these improvements in access to health care and health soon after birth had echoes in the form of large student achievement gains for black teenagers in the 1980's, contributing to the decline in the black-white test score gap. Their results are consistent with improved health care access and early childhood health improving test scores by between 0.7 and 1 standard deviations—a very large impact that implies large increases in lifetime earnings. For example, studying a different intervention Chetty, Friedman, and Rockoff (2011) find the financial value (the net present value at age 12 of the discounted increase in lifetime earnings) of a standard deviation increase in test scores to be $46,190 per grade.

While it may not be surprising that human capital interventions have long-run returns, recent studies have also found intergenerational effects on child outcomes from tax or near-cash transfers to their parents. That is, recent evidence suggests that government transfers that ameliorate child poverty by increasing family income have lasting, long-run benefits in terms of better child outcomes. For example, Hoynes, Schanzenbach, and Almond (2013) study the initial roll-out of the Food Stamp (now, SNAP) program between its initial pilot in 1961 and 1975. While Food Stamps are distributed as vouchers for food purchases, since their amount is generally less than households spend on food the vouchers likely affect family behavior in the same manner as increased cash income (Hoynes and Schanzenbach 2009). Hoynes and coauthors find that exposure to Food Stamps led to improvements in adult health (reductions in the incidence of high blood pressure and obesity) and, for women, increased economic self-sufficiency. Similarly, Dahl and Lochner (2012) and Chetty, Friedman, and Rockoff (2011) find that family receipt of additional income from refundable tax credits improves the achievement test scores of children in the family. Chetty and coauthors estimate that the implied increase in adult earnings due to improved achievement as a child is on the same order of magnitude, and probably greater, than the value of the tax expenditures.

The results discussed above highlight the crucial fact that government expenditures on the safety net have a strong economic justification. Not only do they help to propel struggling adults back onto their feet and protect them and their families from hardship, they improve opportunity and the adult outcomes of their children. As such, the poverty-reducing impact of these programs constitutes an important investment opportunity. To give a sense of the magnitude of this opportunity, Holzer, Schanzenbach, Duncan and Ludwig (2008) estimate the cost of childhood poverty at about $500 billion (in 2007 dollars) or about 4 percent of gross domestic product annually in terms of foregone earnings, increased costs of crime, and higher health expenditures and lower health.

While the Holzer et al. study is correlational (though it attempts to correct for hereditary components of the intergenerational income correlation) the concern over bias in this estimate is overwhelmed by its magnitude. Based on Census Bureau estimates, the total poverty gap—the shortfall between family resources and the SPM poverty thresholds—among all families with children is about $59.8 billion in 2012, or 0.37 percent of GDP. Even if the Holzer et al. estimate was double the "true" causal effect of eliminating child poverty, the benefit would exceed the added costs five-fold. These numbers create a powerful case for renewed efforts to fight poverty.

IV. The Obama Administration's Record and Agenda to Strengthen Economic Security and Increase Opportunity

"The idea that so many children are born into poverty in the wealthiest nation on Earth is heartbreaking enough. But the idea that a child may never be able to escape that poverty because she lacks a decent education or health care, or a community that views her future as their own, that should offend all of us and it should compel us to action. We are a better country than this."

— President Obama, December 4, 2013.

The programs created during the War on Poverty and refined since have provided crucial support to Americans in need. But challenges clearly remain. In 2012, 49.7 million Americans, including 13.4 million children, lived below the poverty line—an unacceptable number in the richest nation in the world. There is clear evidence that antipoverty programs work, and we must redouble our efforts to enhance and strengthen our safety net.

At the same time, we must realize that while antipoverty programs are doing heroic work to lift struggling families from poverty, there is broad consensus among economists that a strong national recovery in the short run, and stronger economic growth in the long run, are necessary to sustain progress in the fight against poverty. Indeed, as our social safety net reinforces the economic benefits of work by supplementing wages for low earners, a strong labor market with jobs available for all is an essential partner in the fight against poverty. Given the growing economic inequality in the past few decades, we must strive for balanced growth that benefits all Americans. To do so, we must ensure that an economic expansion encompasses everyone, and commit to giving all Americans opportunities for lifelong learning and skills development to ensure a broad base of human capital that will be rewarded by good wages.

This section documents the Obama Administration's record in continuing the fight against poverty, and discusses the Administration's proposals to strengthen the safety net and to improve human capital and increase labor market earnings. These comprise a key part of the broader economic strategy to further the recovery and increase growth—all of which combat poverty.

Taking Immediate Action During the Economic Crisis

As the economy was sliding into the Great Recession, the Administration took action to strengthen the safety net and prevent millions of Americans from falling into poverty. The Recovery Act instituted a number of temporary antipoverty measures, including the creation of the Making Work Pay tax credit worth up to $800 for a married couple, a $250 Economic Recovery Payment for Social Security and SSI recipients; unemployment changes including an additional $25 per week (for up to 26 weeks) to regular UI beneficiaries, increased federal funding for the Extended Benefits program, incentives for states to modernize their UI system to reach part-time workers and recent workforce entrants, and reauthorized Emergency Unemployment Compensation; an increase in SNAP benefits; and an expansion of the Community Services Block Grant (CSBG). The Recovery Act also delivered nearly $100 billion to States, school districts, postsecondary institutions, and students to help address budget shortfalls and meet the educational needs of all. This total included $10 billion for the Title I Grants to Local Educational Agencies program, a flagship program of the War on Poverty's Elementary and Secondary Education Act of 1965, which currently serves more than 23 million students in high-poverty schools, helping ensure access to a high-quality public education.

In addition it included expansions in tax credits that were intended to be made permanent. The EITC expansion increased the credit for families with three or more children, reflecting the fact that they have greater needs and higher poverty rates than families with two children. It also reduced the penalty that some low-income families faced when getting married. Together these two provisions benefit about 6 million households a year by an average of $500. In addition, the partial refundability of the child tax credit for working families was expanded, benefiting 12 million families by an average of $800 each. These changes were subsequently extended through 2017 and the President is proposing to make them permanent.

The impact of these emergency measures on poverty was dramatic. From 2007 to 2012, the poverty rate would have risen by 4.8 percentage points if individuals received no income from tax credits and benefits like nutrition assistance and unemployment insurance. This would have been the largest five-year rise in poverty in 50 years. But, when the poverty rate measurement includes tax credits and benefits as part of income, poverty only rose 1.3 percentage points from 2007 to 2012 (see Figure 5 above). By contrast, during the recession of the early 1980s when the safety net was not expanded by as much, poverty rose by 4.7 percentage points from 17.4 percent in 1979 to 22.1 percent in 1982 (as also shown in Figure 5).

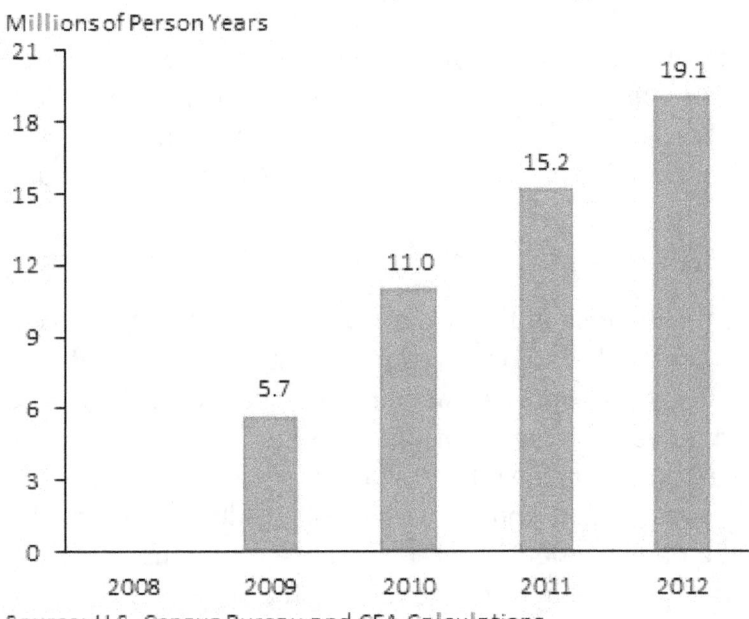

Figure 11

The Antipoverty Impact of ARRA: Cumulative Person Years Kept from Poverty

Source: U.S. Census Bureau and CEA Calculations.

The Recovery Act played a large role in keeping Americans out of poverty during the recession, as shown in Figure 11. In total, between 3.9 and 5.7 million people a year were kept out of poverty by these programs from 2009 to 2012. Without the Recovery Act, the Supplemental Poverty Rate would have been 1.9 percentage points higher in 2009 and 1.7 percentage points higher in 2010. Over the four years between 2009 and 2012, CEA estimates that 19.1 million person years were kept from poverty as a result of the expansions created by the Recovery Act alone. This calculation is conservative, in that it does not account for the impact of those expansions on employment through increased aggregate demand, and does not attempt to measure the impact of other components of the Recovery Act such as increased funding for Pell Grants and paying for COBRA for the unemployed.

Expanding Health Care Security

The Affordable Care Act (ACA) ensures that all Americans have access to quality, affordable health insurance. The ACA provides financial incentives to states to expand their Medicaid programs to all people who are in or near poverty. As a result, 26 states have adopted the Medicaid expansion. For moderate-income Americans, the ACA provides tax credits for the purchase of insurance through marketplaces and cost-sharing reductions. The Congressional Budget Office estimates that, by 2016, these measures will increase the number of Americans with health insurance by 25 million (Congressional Budget Office 2013).

Americans of all income levels are already benefiting from insurance market reforms that ensure access to preventive services and no lifetime coverage limits. Further, Americans buying insurance are no longer forced to pay a higher premium because of their gender or health status, and can be confident that their insurance provides adequate financial protection. The ACA has also begun reforming the way the United States pays for health care to promote more efficiency and quality in the health system, the early results of which are discussed in a recent CEA report (CEA 2013).

Nutrition programs like SNAP are vital to the economic livelihood of many families and communities, especially in a recessionary period. Every time a family uses SNAP benefits to put healthy food on the table, the benefits extend widely beyond those individuals. In fact, the U.S. Department of Agriculture's Economic Research Service estimates that an additional $1 billion in SNAP benefits supports an additional 8,900 to 17,900 full-time-equivalent jobs (Hanson 2010).

Empowering Every Child with a Quality Education

To prepare Americans for the jobs of the future, we have to strengthen our investments in the Nation's educational system. The Administration has invested in coordinated State systems of early learning and proposed new policies building on evidence of how to create a foundation for success in the formative early years of life. High-quality early learning and development programs can help level the playing field for children from lower-income families on vocabulary, social and emotional development, and academic skills while helping students to stay on track and stay engaged in the early elementary grades. These programs generate a significant return on investment for society through a reduced need for spending on other services, such as remedial education, grade repetition, and special education, as well as increased later productivity and earnings. The Administration's comprehensive early-learning agenda invests in early childhood education, care, and development for our nation's youngest learners. In partnership with the States, the Preschool for All initiative would provide high-quality preschool for four-year olds from low- and moderate-income families, while encouraging States to serve additional four-year olds from middle-income families. The Administration has also proposed investments in high-quality early learning for infants and toddlers through new Early Head Start-Child Care Partnerships, as well as an extension and expansion of evidence-based voluntary home visiting programs that allow nurses, social workers, educators, and other professionals to connect pregnant women and vulnerable families with young children to tools that positively impact the child's health, development, and ability to learn.

Over the past 50 years, improvements in education at all levels have produced large returns for many Americans and played a key role in the economic mobility of children born to poor families. Because economic progress and educational achievement are inextricably linked, educating every American student to graduate from high school prepared for college and for a career is a national imperative. The President has articulated a goal for America to once again lead the world in college completion by the year 2020, and the Administration's education efforts aim toward this overarching objective. To provide a high-quality education to all American children, the Administration, in partnership with states, has advanced reforms of the Nation's K-12 education system to support higher standards that will prepare students to succeed in college and the workplace; efforts to recruit, prepare, develop, and advance effective teachers and principals; efforts to eliminate discrimination on the basis of race, color, national origin, sex and disability in public school; efforts to ensure the use of data in the classroom; and a national effort to turn around our chronically lowest-achieving schools. The School Improvement Grants (SIG) program has invested over $5 billion in 1500 of the nation's lowest performing schools. The Promise Neighborhood Program, established by this Administration in 2010, has funded 58 neighborhoods across the country to design comprehensive projects that include a continuum of services and designed to combat the effects of poverty and improve education and life outcomes, from birth through college to career. The Administration has also put forward proposals to redesign the Nation's high schools to better engage students and to connect 99 percent of students to high-speed broadband and digital learning tools within the next five years. Continued investments and reforms are needed to ensure that all students have access to a high-quality education that prepares them for college and a career and for success in today's global economy.

With the average earnings of college graduates at a level twice as high as that of workers with only a high school diploma, higher education is now the clearest pathway into the middle class. Our Nation suffers from a college attainment gap, as high school graduates from the wealthiest families are almost certain to continue on to higher education, while just over half of high school graduates in the poorest quarter of families attend college. This gap has increased over the past several decades. And while more than half of college students graduate within six years, the completion rate for low-income students is around 25 percent. To achieve the President's goal for college completion, ensure that America's students and workers receive the education and training needed for the jobs of today and tomorrow, and provide greater security for the middle class, the Administration is working to make college more accessible, affordable, and attainable for all American families. Under President Obama, Pell Grant funding was increased to serve over 3 million additional low-income students and the average grant was increased by more than $900. The Administration also created the American Opportunity Tax Credit to ease college costs for over 9 million families, and championed comprehensive reform of student loans that will save taxpayers $68 billion over the next decade. Finally, the administration has launched an array of policies to contain college costs, and make it easier for students to manage their student debt through income-based repayment reforms, which limit student loan payments to a percentage of their income so that young workers will not be swamped by debt payments as they are establishing their households and careers.

Given the critical importance of education in expanding skills and opportunities, the Administration implemented several policies designed to increase college access and affordability for low-income students. Recognizing that the opportunity to acquire the skills to get and keep a good job starts early and through education, the President is also proposing to modernize America's high schools for real-world learning. The goal is to provide challenging, relevant experiences, and reward schools that develop new partnerships with colleges and employers, and that create classes that focus on technology, science, engineering, and other skills today's employers are demanding to fill jobs now and in the future.

Creating Jobs and Growing Our Economy

Building on the evidence that well-designed training programs can improve employment and earnings (Andersson et al. 2013), this Administration has proposed investing in subsidized employment and training opportunities for adults who are low-income or long-term unemployed. In 2009 and 2010, 372,000 low-income youth were placed into summer and year-round employment, and supported job opportunities were created for about 260,000 low-income individuals. In addition, the President continues to build public-private partnerships to provide opportunities for low-income youth.

The Administration is using all available tools to help people who have lost their jobs to find new work or to train for new careers in growth fields that will provide better jobs and paths to viable careers. This includes supporting training opportunities that lead directly to a job, and making sure our unemployment system promotes re-employment through wide-ranging reforms to the unemployment insurance program, some of which were adopted in the Middle Class Tax Relief and Jobs Creation Act of 2012, and continued investment in reemployment services, which have proven effective in speeding the return to work.

The President has proposed to build on these successes by further investing in creating job and work-based training opportunities for the long-term unemployed and youth seeking skills and wanting to get into the workplace.

This Administration has already invested $1.5 billion in community college-business partnerships in all 50 states to build capacity and develop curricula to train workers for jobs in growing industries. President Obama has proposed to build on these successes with further investments that will transform community college education and support Americans in getting training to enter skilled jobs.

RAISING THE MINIMUM WAGE

In 2013, the federal minimum wage was at the same inflation-adjusted level as it was in 1950. A full-time worker earning $7.25 per hour would not be able to keep a family of four out of poverty, even with the help of the Earned Income Tax Credit and Child Tax Credit. Instead of allowing the value of the minimum wage to continue to erode while incomes at the top of the distribution soar, it is time to make the minimum wage a wage people can live on.

Raising the minimum wage to $10.10 per hour would help a large, diverse group of workers, and indexing it to inflation would ensure that its real value does not deteriorate over time, as it has after past increases. Nearly 19 million people earned wages near the minimum wage in 2012 and would be directly affected by such an increase, 48 percent of whom had household incomes below $35,000. Full-time workers earning exactly the minimum wage would see their earnings increase by $5,700, enough to move a family of four from 17 percent below the poverty line to 6 percent above it, once tax credit assistance is included. The CEA estimates that raising the minimum wage to $10.10 by 2016 would lift roughly 1.6 million workers whose wages are currently near the minimum wage, and members of their families, out of poverty.

Opponents of increasing the minimum wage argue that the beneficiaries are largely middle-class teenagers, and those most in need of assistance are kept out of jobs by high wages. The available evidence does not support those claims. Among those workers who would be directly affected by increasing the minimum wage to $10.10, 90 percent are more than 18 years old. A large literature has considered the effects of minimum wages on employment, and the best evidence suggests there is little to no effect (Doucouliagos and Stanley 2009). While a higher minimum wage could increase compensation costs for employers, they could also reap benefits, including lower employee turnover rates, and by extension lower costs of hiring and training new workers, as well as increased demand for their goods and services among low-wage workers.

Fighting for Workers

Work that pays enough to support a family is the most central antipoverty measure. In 2013, the Obama Administration finalized rules to extend minimum wage and overtime protections to nearly two million direct-care workers who provide care assistance to elderly people and people with illnesses, injuries, or disabilities. This will ensure our nation's health aides, personal care aides and certified nursing assistants receive the same basic protections already provided to most U.S. workers, while improving the quality and stability of care for those who rely on them.

Minimum wage and overtime protections have been a bulwark of protection against poverty, but the minimum wage has not kept pace with inflation. Today, a worker trying to support a family on the minimum wage is still living in poverty. That is why President Obama supports the Harkin-Miller bill to increase the minimum wage to $10.10 by 2016 (see box).

Investing in and Rebuilding Hard-Hit Communities

Living in a high-poverty area presents a wide variety of challenges, including crime, limited access to quality education, and scarcity of good jobs. Since these issues often interact with each other and compound the problems they create individually, it is very difficult for people, particularly children, to overcome the disadvantages created by and associated with poverty.

A child's zip code should never determine his or her destiny. To help provide ladders of opportunity so that every child has a chance to succeed, the Administration is working with State and local governments to focus public and private resources on transforming areas of high need into communities of opportunity.

The Administration's Promise Zones initiative focuses existing government resources on competitively selected communities and leverages private investment to create jobs, improve public safety, increase educational opportunities, and provide affordable housing. The Obama Administration will designate 20 communities over the next several years with this intense and layered approach to community revitalization.

That approach includes working with local leadership, and bringing to bear the resources of the President's signature revitalization initiatives from the Department of Education (ED), the Department of Housing and Urban Development (HUD), the Department of Agriculture, and the Department of Justice (DOJ), to ensure that federal programs and resources support the efforts to turn around 20 of the highest poverty urban, rural and tribal communities across the country.

The Promise Zones initiative will build on existing programs, including the Department of HUD's Choice Neighborhoods and the Department of Education's Promise Neighborhoods grant programs. The Administration has invested $248 million in Choice and $157 million in Promise since 2010. For every federal dollar spent, Choice Neighborhoods has attracted eight dollars of private and other investment and has developed nearly 100,000 units of mixed-income housing in 260 communities, ensuring that low-income residents can afford to continue living in their communities. Promise Neighborhoods grants are supporting approximately 50 communities representing more than 700 schools. To help leverage and sustain grant work, 1,000 national, state, and community organizations have signed-on to partner with a Promise Neighborhood site. By expanding these programs, the Administration continues to support local efforts to transform low-income urban, rural, and tribal communities across the country.

V. Conclusion

The War on Poverty represented a dramatic shift in the Federal Government's priorities for helping those who are left behind in a growing economy. It set in motion a series of changes that transformed our social safety net and improved the well-being and economic outcomes of countless low-income Americans and their children. The architects of the War on Poverty believed that the combined effect of government policies attacking poverty on many fronts— providing income when earnings are low, providing access to health insurance, insuring that people have shelter and a minimal food budget, and providing access to education at all ages— would dramatically raise employment and earnings and reduce material hardship. In the years since 1964, this optimism and belief in the capacity of government to improve the lives of less fortunate Americans has at times given way to the cynical belief that the safety net is ineffective, or even exacerbates the problems of the poor by reducing the incentives for those able to work to do so.

The most important lesson from the War on Poverty is that government programs and policies *can* lift people from poverty; indeed they *have* for the past 50 years. Poverty rates fell from 25.8 percent in 1967 to 16 percent in 2012—a decline of nearly 40 percent. In 2012 alone, the combined effect of all federal tax, cash and in-kind aid programs was to lift approximately 14.5 percent of the population—over 45 million people—out of poverty.

But another lesson is that we cannot afford to simply embrace any program that purports to achieve this goal or attempt to freeze them in time. Instead, our antipoverty efforts have benefited from enormous changes in public policy since the 1960s, informed by a wealth of research on both successful and failed programs that provide important insights into what does and does not work in fighting poverty. Our safety net has evolved to put more emphasis on rewarding and supporting work, such as by providing greater support to working families through the Earned Income Tax Credit and refundable Child Tax Credit, while also making it easier for them to get help from programs like SNAP and Medicaid. In 1967 we spent $19 billion in today's dollars on what was then called AFDC and nothing on the Earned Income Tax Credit. Today the Earned Income Tax Credit and partially refundable Child Tax Credit are 3.8 times the size of the TANF program.[22] Meanwhile, the Affordable Care Act advances the goal of providing quality affordable health care to all Americans, with financial incentives to states to expand their Medicaid programs to all people who are in or near poverty and generous tax credits for moderate-income households. Our safety net remains imperfect, but these reforms and improvements represent important progress—and they also help many families work and raise the rewards to that work.

Nearly 50 million Americans still live in poverty, however, including 13.4 million children, and so there remains a need to do more to help the poor. The 1964 Economic Report of the President estimated that the total shortfall in income necessary to bring all poor families up to the

---

[22] Based on CEA calculations using data from
http://www.whitehouse.gov/sites/default/files/omb/budget/fy2014/assets/hist.pdf.

poverty level was $11 billion (about $71 billion in today's dollars), or about 1.6 percent of the country's annual Gross Domestic Product. Our nation has grown much richer since, and today the total shortfall below poverty is only 0.6 percent of GDP. Continuing to make progress in closing that shortfall will require not just defending the programs that have helped reduce poverty but also continuing the efforts to strengthen the economy, increase growth and ensure that growth is reflected in broad-based wage gains so that families lift themselves out of poverty.

References

Acs, Gregory and Seth Zimmerman. 2008. "U.S. Intragenerational Economic Mobility from 1984-2004: Trends and Implications." Washington, DC: The Pew Charitable Trusts.

Almond, Douglas, Kenneth Y. Chay, and Michael Greenstone. 2006. "Civil Rights, the War on Poverty, and Black-White Convergence in Infant Mortality in the Rural South and Mississippi." MIT Department of Economics Working Paper 07-04.

Anderson, Michael L. 2008. "Multiple Inference and Gender Differences in the Effects of Early Intervention: A Reevaluation of the Abecedarian, Perry Preschool, and Early Training Projects." *Journal of the American Statistical Association* 103, no. 484: 1481-1495.

Andersson, Fredrik, Harry J. Holzer, Julia I. Lane, David Rosenblum and Jeffrey Smith. 2013. "Does Federally-Funded Job Training Work? Nonexperimental Estimates of WIA Training Impacts Using Longitudinal Data on Workers and Firms," NBER Working Papers 19446, National Bureau of Economic Research, Inc.

Anzick, Michael A. and David A. Weaver. 2001. "Reducing Poverty Among Elderly Women." Working Paper Series Number 87. Washington, D.C.: Office of Research, Evaluation, and Statistics, Social Security Administration.

Auten, Gerald, Geoffrey Gee, and Nicholas Turner. 2013. "Income Inequality, Mobility, and Turnover at the Top in the US, 1987–2010." *American Economic Review 103 (May, Papers and Proceedings, 2012): 168–172.*

Baicker, Katherine, Sarah L. Taubman, Heidi L. Allen, Mira Bernstein, Jonathan H. Gruber, Joseph P. Newhouse, Eric C. Schneider, Bill J. Wright, Alan M. Zaslavsky, and Amy N. Finkelstein. 2013a. "The Oregon Experiment—Effects of Medicaid on Clinical Outcomes." *The New England Journal of Medicine* 368: 1713-1722.

Ben-Shalom, Yonatan, Robert A. Moffitt, and John Karl Scholz. 2011. "An Assessment of Anti-Poverty Programs in the United States." Working Paper 17042. Cambridge, Mass.: National Bureau of Economic Research.

Björklund, Anders, Markus Jäntti, and Gary Solon. 2005. "Influences of Nature and Nurture on Earnings Variation: A Report on a Study of Various Sibling Types in Sweden." In *Unequal Chances: Family Background and Economic Success,* edited by Samuel Bowles, Herbert Gintis, and Melissa Osborne Groves, pp. 145-164. Princeton University Press.

Black, Sandra E. and Paul J. Devereux. 2011. "Recent Developments in Intergenerational Mobility." In *Handbook of Labor Economics,* Volume 4B, edited by Orley Ashenfelter and David Card, pp. 1487–1541. North Holland.

Blank, Rebecca M. 1993. "Public Sector Growth and Labor Market Flexibility: The United States vs. the United Kingdom." Working Paper 4338. Cambridge, Mass.: National Bureau of Economic Research.

_____. 2000. "Fighting Poverty: Lessons from Recent U.S. History." *Journal of Economic Perspectives* 14, no. 2: 3-19.

_____. 2007. "Improving the Safety Net for Single Mothers Who Face Serious Barriers to Work." *Future of Children* 17, no. 2: 183-197.

Burtless, Gary. 1986. "Social Security, Unanticipated Benefit Increases, and the Timing of Retirement." *Review of Economic Studies* 53, no. 5: 781-805.

Cancian, Maria and Deborah Reed. 2009. "Family structure, childbearing, and parental employment: Implications for the level and trend in poverty." *Focus* 26, no.2: 21-26.

Campbell, Frances A., Barbara H. Wasik, Elizabeth Pungello, Margaret Burchinal, Oscar Barbarin, Kirsten Kainz, Joseph J. Sparling, and Craig T. Ramey. 2008. "Young Adult Outcomes of the Abecedarian and CARE Early Childhood Educational Interventions." *Early Childhood Research Quarterly* 23, no. 4: 452–466.

Caplow, Theodore and Jonathan Simon. 1999. "Understanding Prison Policy and Population Trends." *Crime and Justice* 26: 63-120.

Card, David E. and Steven Raphael. 2013. *Immigration, Poverty, and Socioeconomic Inequality.* New York: Russell Sage.

Census Bureau. 2013. "Poverty – Experimental Measures." http://www.census.gov/hhes/povmeas/data/nas/tables/index.html

Chay, Kenneth Y., Jonathan Guryan, and Bhashkar Mazumder. 2009. "Birth Cohort and the Black-White Achievement Gap: The Roles of Access and Health Soon After Birth." Working Paper No. 15078. Cambridge, Mass., National Bureau of Economic Research.

Chetty, Raj. 2008. "Moral Hazard versus Liquidity and Optimal Unemployment Insurance." *Journal of Political Economy* 116, no. 2: 173-234.

Chetty, Raj, John N. Friedman, and Jonah E. Rockoff. 2011. "New Evidence on the Long-Term Impacts of Tax Credits." Statistics of Income Paper Series. Internal Revenue Service.

Chetty, Raj, John N. Friedman, and Emmanuel Saez. 2012. "Using Differences in Knowledge Across Neighborhoods to Uncover the Impacts of the EITC on Earnings." Working Paper 18232. Cambridge, Mass.: National Bureau of Economic Research.

Chetty, Raj, John N. Friedman, Soren Leth-Peterson, Torben Heien Nielson, and Tore Olsen. 2013. "Subsidies vs. Nudges: Which Policies Increase Saving the Most?" Issue Brief 13-3. Center for Retirement Research at Boston College.

Chetty,Raj, Nathaniel Hendren, Patrick Kline, and Emmanuel Saez. 2014. "Where is the Land of Opportunity? The Geography of Intergenerational Mobility in the United States." Harvard University Working Paper.

Congressional Budget Office. 2013. "Growth in Means-Tested Programs and Tax Credits for Low-Income Households." http://www.cbo.gov/sites/default/files/cbofiles/attachments/43934-Means-TestedPrograms.pdf.

Connelly, Rachel and Jean Kimmel. 2003. "The Effect of Child Care Costs on the Employment and Welfare Recipiency of Single Mothers." *Southern Economic Journal* 69, no. 3: 498-519.

Corak, Miles. 2006. "Do Poor Children Become Poor Adults? Lessons from a Cross Country Comparison of Generational Earnings Mobility." IZA Discussion Paper No. 1993.

_____. 2011. "Inequality from generation to generation: the United States in Comparison." Graduate School of Public and International Affairs, University of Ottawa.

Corcoran, Mary. 2001. "Mobility, Persistence, and the Consequences of Child Poverty for Children: Child and Adult Outcomes." In *Understanding Poverty*, edited by Sheldon H. Danziger and Robert H. Haveman, pp. 127-140. Cambridge, Mass: Harvard University Press.

Corcoran, Mary and Terry Adams. 1997. "Race, Sex, and the Intergenerational Transmission of Poverty." In *Consequences of Growing Up Poor*, edited by Greg J. Duncan and Jeanne Brooks-Gunn, pp. 461-517. New York: Russell Sage Foundation.

Council of Economic Advisers. 1964. Economic Report of the President. Washington, D.C.: Council of Economic Advisers, Executive Office of the President.

Council of Economic Advisers. 2013. "Trends in Health Care and Cost Growth and the Role of the Affordable Care Act." November.

Dahl, Gordon B. and Lance Lochner. 2012. "The Impact of Family Income on Child Achievement: Evidence from the Earned Income Tax Credit." *American Economic Review* 102, no. 5: 1927-1956.

Danziger, Sheldon H., Lesley J. Turner, and Kristin S. Seefeldt. 2006. "Failing the Transition from Welfare to Work: Women Chronically Disconnected from Employment and Cash Welfare." *Social Science Quarterly* 87, no. 2: 227-249.

Deming, David. 2009. "Early Childhood Intervention and Life-Cycle Skill Development: Evidence from Head Start." *American Economic Journal: Applied Economics* 1, no. 3: 111-134.

DiNardo, John, Nicole M. Fortin, and Thomas Lemieux. 1996. "Labor Market Institutions and the Distribution of Wages, 1973-1992: A Semiparametric Approach." *Econometrica* 64, no. 5: 1001-1044.

DiNardo, John, and Thomas Lemieux. 1997. "Diverging Male Wage Inequality in the United States and Canada, 1981-1988: Do Institutions Explain the Difference?." *Industrial and Labor Relations Review* 50, no. 4: 629-651.

Dowd, Tim and John B. Horowitz. 2011. "Income Mobility and the Earned Income Tax Credit: Short-Term Safety Net or Long-Term Income Support." *Public Finance Review* 39, no. 5: 619-652.

Doucouliagos, Hirstos and T.D. Stanley. 2009. "Publication Selection Bias in Minimum-Wage Research? A Meta-Regression Analysis." *British Journal of Industrial Relations* 47, no. 2: 406-428.

Dube, Arindrajit, T. William Lester, and Michael Reich. 2010. "Minimum Wage Effects Across State Borders: Estimates Using Contiguous Counties." *The Review of Economics and Statistics* 92, no. 4: 945-964.

Dube, Arindrajit. 2013. "Minimum Wages and the Distribution of Family Incomes." Working Paper. https://dl.dropboxusercontent.com/u/15038936/Dube_MinimumWagesFamilyIncomes.pdf.

Duncan, Greg J., Katherine Magnuson, Ariel Kalil, Kathleen Ziol-Guest. 2012. "The Importance of Early Childhood Poverty." *Social Indicators Research* 108, no. 1: pp 87-98.

Council of Economic Advisers. 1964. *Economic Report of the President*. Washington, D.C.: Government Printing Office.

Eissa, Nada and Hilary W. Hoynes. 2005. "Behavioral Responses to Taxes: Lessons from the EITC and Labor Supply." Working Paper 11729. Cambridge, Mass.: National Bureau of Economic Research.

Eissa, Nada and Jeffrey B. Liebman. 1996. "Labor Supply Response to the Earned Income Tax Credit." *The Quarterly Journal of Economics* 111, no. 2: 605-637.

Engelhardt, Gary V., and Jonathan Gruber. 2006. "Social Security and the Evolution of Elderly Poverty." In *Public Policy and the Income Distribution*, edited by Alan J. Auerbach, David E. Card, and John M. Quigley, pp. 259-287. New York: Russell Sage Foundation.

Fisher, Gordon M. 1992. "The Development and History of the Poverty Thresholds." *Social Security Bulletin* 55, no. 4: 3-14.

Fox, Liana, Irwin Garfinkel, Neeraj Kaushal, Jane Waldfogel, and Christopher Wimer. 2013. "Waging War on Poverty: Historical Trends in Poverty Using the Supplemental Poverty Measure." Working Paper 13-01. Columbia Population Research Center.

Fremstad, Shawn. 2009. "Half in Ten: Why Taking Disability into Account is Essential to Reducing Income Poverty and Expanding Economic Inclusion." Reports and Issue Briefs 2009-30. Washington, D.C.: Center for Economic and Policy Research.

Garces, Eliana, Duncan Thomas, and Janet Currie. 2002. "Longer-Term Effects of Head Start." *American Economic Review* 92, no. 4: 999–1012.

Gibbs, Chloe, Jens Ludwig, and Douglas L. Miller. 2013. "Head Start Origins and Impacts." In *Legacies of the War on Poverty*, edited by Martha Bailey and Sheldon Danziger, pp. 39-65. New York: Russell Sage Foundation Press.

Gottschalk, Peter and Sheldon Danziger. 2003. "Wage Inequality, Earnings Inequality and Poverty in the U.S. Over the Last Quarter of the Twentieth Century." Working Papers in Economics 560. Boston College Department of Economics.

Danziger, Sheldon and Peter Gottschalk. 1995. *America Unequal*. Harvard University Press.

Hanson, Kenneth. 2010. "The Food Assistance National Income-Output Multiplier (FANIOM) Model and Stimulus Effects of SNAP." Economic Research Report No. 103. United States Department of Agriculture Economic Research Service.

Harrington, Michael. 1962. *The Other America*. New York: Simon and Schuster.

Heckman, James J. and Dimitriy V. Masterov. 2007. "The Productivity Argument for Investing in Young Children." *Applied Economic Perspectives and Policy* 29, no. 3: 446-493.

Heckman, James J., Seong Hyeok Moon, Rodrigo Pinto, Peter A. Savelyev, Adam Yavitz. 2009. "The Rate of Return to the High/Scope Perry Preschool Program." Working Paper No. 15471. Cambridge, Mass.: National Bureau of Economic Research.

Heckman, James J., Seong Hyeok Moon, Rodrigo Pinto, Peter Savelyev, and Adam Yavitz. 2010. "A New Cost-Benefit and Rate of Return Analysis for the Perry Preschool Program: A Summary." Working Paper No. 16180. Cambridge, Mass.: National Bureau of Economic Research.

Heckman, James J., Rodrigo Pinto, Azeem M. Shaikh, and Adam Yavitz. 2011. "Inference with Imperfect Randomization: the Case of the Perry Preschool Program." Working Paper No. 16935. Cambridge, Mass.: National Bureau of Economic Research.

Holzer, Harry J. 2007. "Collateral Costs: The Effects of Incarceration on the Employment and Earnings of Young Workers." IZA Discussion Paper No. 3118.

Holzer, Harry J., Diane Whitmore Schanzenbach, Greg J. Duncan, and Jens Ludwig. 2008. "The Economic Costs of Childhood Poverty in the United States." *Journal of Children and Poverty* 14, no. 1: 41-61.

Hotz, V. Joseph and John Karl Scholz. 2003. "The Earned Income Tax Credit." In *Means-Tested Transfer Programs in the U.S.*, edited by Robert A. Moffitt, pp. 141-198. Chicago: University of Chicago Press.

Hoynes, Hilary W., Marianne E. Page, and Ann Huff Stevens. 2006. "Poverty in America: Trends and Explanations." *Journal of Economic Perspectives* 92, no. 3: 748-765.

Hoynes, Hilary W. and Diane W. Schanzenbach. 2009. "Consumption Reponses to In-Kind Transfers: Evidence from the Introduction of the Food Stamp Program." *American Economic Journal: Applied Economics* 1, no. 4: 109-139.

_____. 2012. "Work incentives and the Food Stamp Program." *Journal of Public Economics* 96, no. 1: 151-162.

Hoynes, Hilary W., Diane W. Schanzenbach, and Douglas Almond. 2012. "Long Run Impacts of Childhood Access to the Safety Net." Working Paper 18535. Cambridge, Mass.: National Bureau of Economic Research.

Ichino, Andrea, Loukas Karabarbounis, and Enrico Moretti. 2009. "The Political Economy of Intergenerational Income Mobility." IZA Discussion Paper No. 4767.

Isaacs, Julia B. 2008. "Economic Mobility of Families across Generations." In *Getting Ahead or Losing Ground: Economic Mobility in America*, Julia Isaacs, Isabel Sawhill and Ron Haskins. Washington D.C.: The Pew Charitable Trusts.

Isaacs, Julia B., Isabel Sawhill, and Ron Haskins. 2008. *Getting Ahead or Losing Ground: Economic Mobility in America.* Washington, D.C.: Brookings Institution.

Jacob, Brian A. and Jens Ludwig. 2012. "The Effects of Housing Assistance on Labor Supply: Evidence from a Voucher Lottery." *American Economic Review* 102, no. 1: 272-304.

Jäntti, Markus, Bernt Bratsberg, Knut Røed, Oddbjørn Raaum, Robin Naylor, Eva Österbacka, Anders Björklund, and Tor Eriksson. 2006. "American Exceptionalism in a New Light: A Comparison of Intergenerational Earnings Mobility in the Nordic Countries, the United Kingdom and the United States." IZA Discussion Paper No. 1938.

Johnson, Rucker C. 2008. "Ever-increasing Levels of Parental Incarceration and the Consequences for Children." In *Do Prisons Make us Safer?*, ed. S. Raphael and M. Stoll, 177-206. Russell Sage Foundation.

Korenman and Remler. 2013. "Rethinking Elderly Poverty: Time for a Health Inclusive Poverty Measure?" NBER Working Paper 18900, National Bureau of Economic Research.

Lee, Chul-In and Gary Solon, 2009. "Trends in Intergenerational Income Mobility," *The Review of Economics and* Statistics, 91, no. 4: 766-772

Lee, David S. 1999. "Wage Inequality in the United States During the 1980s: Rising Dispersion or Falling Minimum Wage?" *Quarterly Journal of Economics* 114, no. 3: 977-1023.

Lemieux, Thomas. 2008. "The Changing Nature of Wage Inequality." *Journal of Population Economics* 21, no. 1: 21-48.

Liebman, Jeffrey B. 1998. "The Impact of the Earned Income Tax Credit on Incentives and Income Distribution." In *Tax Policy and the Economy, Volume 12,* edited by James M. Poterba, pp. 83-120. Cambridge, Mass.: National Bureau of Economic Research.

Ludwig, Jens and Douglas Miller. 2007. "Does Head Start Improve Children's Life Chances? Evidence from a Regression Discontinuity Design." *Quarterly Journal of Economics* 122, no. 1: 159-208.

Matsudaira, Jordan D. and Rebecca M. Blank. 2013. "The Impact of Earnings Disregards on the Behavior of Low-Income Families." *Journal of Policy Analysis and Management* 33, no. 1: 7-35.

Mayer, Susan E. and Leonard M. Lopoo. 2008. "Government Spending and Intergenerational Mobility." *Journal of Public Economics* 92, no. 1-2: 139-158.

Mayer, Susan E. 1997. *What Money Can't Buy: Family Income and Children's Life Chances*. Cambridge, MA: Harvard University Press.

Meyer, Bruce D., Wallace K. C. Mok, and James X. Sullivan. 2009. "The Underreporting of Transfers in Household Surveys: Its Nature and Consequences." Working Paper 15181. Cambridge, Mass.: National Bureau of Economic Research.

Meyer, Bruce D. and Dan T. Rosenbaum. 2001. "Welfare, the Earned Income Tax Credit, and the Labor Supply of Single Mothers." *Quarterly Journal of Economics* 116, no. 3: 1063-1114.

Meyer, Bruce D. and James X. Sullivan. 2003. "Measuring the Well-Being of the Poor Using Income and Consumption." Journal of Human Resources 38, Supplement: 1180-1220.

Meyer, Bruce D. and James X. Sullivan. 2012a. "Winning the War: Poverty from the Great Society to the Great Recession." *Brookings Papers on Economic Activity* 45, no. 2: 133-200.

Meyer, Bruce D. and James X. Sullivan. 2012b. "Identifying the Disadvantaged: Official Poverty, Consumption Poverty, and the New Supplemental Poverty Measure." Journal of Economic Perspectives 26, no. 3: 111-136.

Meyer, Bruce D. and James X. Sullivan. 2013. "Winning the War: Poverty from the Great Society to the Great Recession." Working Paper 18718. Cambridge, Mass.: National Bureau of Economic Research.

Mishel, Lawrence, Josh Bivens, Elise Gould, and Heidi Shierholz. The State of Working America, 12th Edition. A forthcoming Economic Policy Institute book. Ithaca, N.Y.: Cornell University Press.

Misra, Joya, Michelle Budig, and Irene Boeckmann. 2011. "Work-Family Policies and the Effects of Children on Women's Employment Hours and Wages." *Community, Work and Family* 14, no. 2: 139-157.

Nicholson-Crotty, Sean and Kenneth J. Meier. 2003. "Crime and Punishment: The Politics of Federal Criminal Justice Sanctions." *Political Research Quarterly* 56, no. 2: 119-126.

Orshansky, Mollie. 1965. "Counting the Poor: Another Look at the Poverty Profile." *Social Security Bulletin* 28, no. 1: 3-29.

Peri, Giovanni. 2013. "Immigrant Workers, Native Poverty and Labor Market Competition." *Policy Brief, Center for Poverty Research* 1, no. 3.

Peters, Alan H. and Peter S. Fisher. 2002. "State Enterprise Zones: Have They Worked?" Kalamazoo, MI: W.E. Upjohn Institute for Employment Research Press.

Piketty, Thomas and Emmanuel Saez. 2003. "Income Inequality in the United States, 1913-1998." *Quarterly Journal of Economics* 118, no. 1: 1-39.

Raphael, Steven. 2007. "Early Incarceration Spells and the Transition to Adulthood." In *The Price of Independence: The Economics of Early Adulthood*, edited by Sheldon Danziger and Cecilia Elena Rouse, pp. 278-306. New York: Russell Sage Foundation.

Reed, Deborah and Maria Cancian. 2001. "Sources of Inequality: Measuring the Contributions of Income Sources to Rising Family Income Inequality." *Review of Income and Wealth* 47, no. 3: 321-333.

Sawhill, Isabel V. and John E. Morton. 2007. "Economic Mobility: Is the American Dream Alive and Well?" Washington, D.C.: Economic Mobility Project, Pew Charitable Trusts.

Schur, Lisa A., Douglas L. Kruse, and Peter Blanck. 2013. *People with Disabilities: Sidelined or Mainstreamed?* Cambridge, England: Cambridge University Press.

Schweinhart, Lawrence J., Jeanne Montie, Zongping Xiang, W. Steven Barnett, Clive R. Belfield, and Milagros Nores. 2005. *Lifetime Effects: The High/Scope Perry Preschool Study Through Age 40*. Monographs of the High/Scope Educational Research Foundation. Ypsilanti, MI: High/Scope Press.

Sen, Amartya. 2009. *The Idea of Justice.* London: Allen Lane.

Singh, Gopal K. and Michael D. Kogan. 2007. "Persistent Socioeconomic Disparities in Infant, Neonatal, and Postneonatal Mortality Rates in the United States, 1969-2001." *Pediatrics* 119, no. 4: 928-939.

Sharkey, Patrick. 2009. "Neighborhoods and the Black-White Mobility Gap." Washington, D.C.: Economic Mobility Project, Pew Charitable Trusts.

She, Peiyun and Gina A. Livermore. 2007. "Material Hardship, Poverty, and Disability Among Working-Age Adults." *Social Science Quarterly* 88, no. 4: 970-989.

Sherman, Arloc. 2013. "Official Poverty Measure Masks Gains Made Over Last 50 Years." Center on Budget and Policy Priorities. http://www.cbpp.org/files/9-13-13pov.pdf.

Short, Kathleen. 2012. "The Research Supplemental Poverty Measure: 2011" Current Population Reports. November.

Short, Kathleen. 2013. "The Research Supplemental Poverty Measure: 2012" Current Population Reports. November.

Solon, Gary. 2002. "Cross-Country Differences in Intergenerational Earnings Mobility." *Journal of Economic Perspectives* 16, no. 3: 59– 66.

SRI International. 1983. "Final Report of the Seattle/Denver Income Maintenance Experiment. Vol 1: Design and Results." Menlo Park, CA.

SSA. 2012. *Income of the Population 55 or Older, 2010*. SSA Publication No. 13-11871. Washington, D.C.: Social Security Administration.

Western, Bruce. 2002. "The Impact of Incarceration on Wage Mobility and Inequality." *American Sociological Review* 67: 526-46.

Western, Bruce and Becky Pettit. 2010. "Incarceration and Social Inequality." *Daedalus* 139: 8-19.

Wimer, Christopher, Liana Fox, Irwin Garfinkel, Neeraj Kaushal, and Jane Waldfogel. 2013. "Trends in Poverty with an Anchored Supplemental Poverty Measure." Working Paper 1-25. Columbia Population Research Center.